Chance
Encounters

Chance Encounters: Probability in Games and Simulations was developed by the following people on the *Seeing and Thinking Mathematically* project at Education Development Center, Inc.

Project Director	**Project Manager**
Glenn Kleiman	Karen Zweig
Curriculum Developers	**Formative Researchers**
Amy Brodesky	Rebecca Brown
Glenn Kleiman	Shelley Isaacson
Muffie Wiebe	Kristen Mathes
Major Contributors	**Reviewers**
E. Paul Goldenberg	Dan Brutlag
David Schaffer	Al Cuoco
Kimberly Smart	Kristen Herbert
	Charles Lovitt (Curriculum Corp.)
Editor	Susan Janssen
Dan Tobin	Marlene Kliman
	Marianne Thompson
Graphic Production	Bernie Zubrowski
Ellen Smith	
	Administrative Assistant
	Andrea Tench

Teacher Consultants

Robert Bates, Brookline Public Schools, MA
Carol Martignetti Boswell, Arlington Public Schools, MA
Arlene Geller-Petrini, Brookline Public Schools, MA
Sonya Grodberg, Newton Public Schools, MA
Patricia Jorsling, Boston Public Schools, MA
Pat Maloney, Waltham Public Schools, MA
Fran Ostrander, Brookline Public Schools, MA
Mark Rubel, Newton Public Schools, MA

Acknowledgments

We express our appreciation to the following people who contributed to the development of the unit: Debb Clay, Dwyer Middle School, CA; Laurie Cook, Los Alisos Intermediate School, CA; Karan Davies, Clifton Middle School, CA; Jane Fesler, Lakeview Jr. High, CA; Karen Gartland, Lesley College, MA; Tony Guarante, Belmont Public Schools, MA; Hilde Howatch, Retired Mathematics Coordinator, Albuquerque Public Schools, NM; Kate Kowalski, Brookline Public Schools, MA; Joan Martin, Mathematics Coordinator, Newton Public Schools, MA; Diane Mazurie, Hewes Middle School, CA; Barbara McEvoy, Watertown Public Schools, MA; Carol Piercy, Alta Sierra Intermediate School, CA; Steve Porretta, Arlington Public Schools, MA; and Rhonda Weinstein, Mathematics Coordinator, Brookline Public Schools, MA.
We would like to thank all the teachers and students who field tested the unit. We would also like to thank Marlene Nelson, EDC staff photographer.

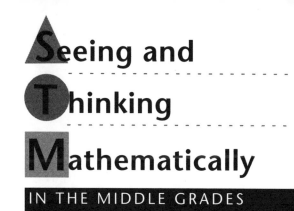

Seeing and
Thinking
Mathematically

IN THE MIDDLE GRADES

Chance Encounters

Probability in Games and Simulations

CREATED BY
EDUCATION DEVELOPMENT CENTER, INC.

Heinemann

A division of Reed Elsevier Inc.
361 Hanover Street   Portsmouth, NH 03801-3912
Offices and agents throughout the world

This project is based at Education Development Center, Inc. (EDC), 55 Chapel Street, Newton, MA, 02158, and was supported, in part, by the National Science Foundation (Grant No. 9054677). Opinions expressed are those of the authors and not necessarily those of the Foundation. The project is developing new mathematics curriculum materials for grades six through eight, and this unit is one of a series of transition units designed to fully address current standards and recommendations for teaching middle school mathematics.

Every effort has been made to contact the copyright holders for permission to reprint borrowed material where necessary. We regret any oversights that may have occurred and would be happy to rectify them in future printings of this work.

Material for Lesson 5 is adapted from *Get It Together: Math Problems for Groups*, Grades 4–12, an EQUALS, Lawrence Hall of Science publication. Copyright 1989 by the Regents of the University of California. Used by permission.

The advertisement in Reproducible 9 *Hoping for Snow* is reprinted by permission from Carol, The Gold Lady, Ltd. Copyright 1993.

Library of Congress Cataloging-in-Publication Data

Chance encounters : probability in games and simulations / created by
    Education Development Center, Inc.
        p.   cm. — (Seeing and thinking mathematically in the middle
grades)
      ISBN 0–435–08351–1 (acid-free)
      1. Probabilities.   I. Education Development Center.   II. Series.
    QA273.C485   1995
    795'.01'5192—dc20   94-42166
                                                                        CIP

Acquired for Heinemann by Toby Gordon and Leigh Peake
Produced by J. B. Tranchemontagne
Copyedited by Alan Huisman
Text Design by Jenny Jensen Greenleaf
Cover Design by Jenny Jensen Greenleaf and Darci Mehall
Cover artwork by Rachel Feuer-Beck, 7th grade, Brookline
Public Schools, MA
Spanish translation by Jaime Fatás Cabeza

Printed in the United States of America on acid-free paper
99 98 97 96 95 VG 1 2 3 4 5 6 7 8 9 10

Contents

Foreword

With the Seeing and Thinking Mathematically (STM) materials, students learn mathematics by doing mathematics, by using and connecting mathematical ideas, and by actively constructing their own understandings. As a teacher, you'll find that these materials will put you closer to your goal of an inviting, exploratory classroom in which all students gain mathematical power. They are designed to help you as a sixth-, seventh-, or eighth-grade mathematics teacher accomplish the following goals.

Improve Your Mathematics Teaching

The reforms in mathematics education advocated by the National Council of Teachers of Mathematics (NCTM), the Mathematical Sciences Education Board (MSEB), and innovative state and local boards of education are challenging to implement in the classroom. The STM materials will support you as you carry out this reform, and are a step in the transition to a new curriculum that will prepare students for the complex technological world in which they will live and work.

Convey the Universal Importance of Mathematics

The STM materials center on the importance of mathematics in the human experience. In STM units, students use mathematics to accomplish things that have been important to all people in all places and all times: to design and build, to predict and plan, to analyze and decide, to imagine and create, to explore and understand, to play and invent, and to formalize and systematize their knowledge. This approach allows students to gain a deep understanding of central mathematical ideas, patterns, representations, proportional reasoning, functions, and mathematical models.

Employ an Innovative, Hands-On Approach to Teaching and Learning

In each STM unit, your students will actively explore mathematical ideas using physical and pictorial models, and will apply these ideas in investigations and projects. Students pose their own problems; create their own strategies; build on their own knowledge and language; and reflect on their work by discussing and writing about it. In the process, they will build "mathematical habits of mind." They will visualize, represent, calculate, compute, model, invent, prove, systematize, and communicate about mathematics.

Provide Opportunities for All Your Students to be Successful with Mathematics

The STM materials provide opportunities for students from different backgrounds to contribute their ideas and experiences, thereby enhancing the mathematical learning experience for everyone in your class. They allow students to use and build on their own strengths and to deepen and broaden their areas of expertise.

Adapt Materials to Meet the Needs of Your Students

Each unit provides a rich set of resources that you can adapt to suit your classroom and teaching style. The lesson plans suggest variations and extensions and include "From the Classroom" vignettes from teachers who have taught the unit.

Employ New Approaches to Assessment

Performance assessment alternatives such as global scoring rubrics, portfolios, and student journals are embedded within the flow of STM learning activities.

Create a Community of Mathematics Learning

The STM units provide opportunities for your students to learn from one another as well as from you. In the STM approach, you become a resource guide, directing, encouraging, and supporting your students' learning.

Engage Your Students in Authentic and Exciting Mathematical Work

In an STM classroom, mathematics is placed in relevant contexts, so that it has a purpose and a motivation. Your students will produce things they value and want to share—products that reflect their own mathematical discoveries.

Build Connections to Other Disciplines and to Your Students' Nonschool Lives

STM units can be connected to all subject areas—art, literature, history, science, and social studies. By using mathematics to analyze, to decide, to plan, to design, and to create, your students will find that mathematics is useful in their everyday lives.

Unit at a Glance

In this unit, students explore key concepts in probability and statistics as they test, revise, and design games and simulations.

Grade Level
6–7

Length
Approximately 25 class periods

Prerequisites
Familiarity with common fractions (halfs, fourths, thirds)

Familiarity with common percents (25%, 50%, 75%, 100%)

Familiarity with common decimals (.1, .25, .5, .75, etc.)

Materials Required
Number cubes

Coins

Spinners

Worksheets and transparencies made from blackline masters provided in the unit

Mathematical Themes
Theoretical and experimental probability

Multiple representations of probability

Modeling situations with simulations

Specific Mathematical Topics
Developing an understanding of randomness, natural variability, and the law of large numbers

Conducting probability experiments

Determining theoretical probabilities

Representing probabilities numerically as fractions, percents, decimals, and ratios

Organizing, representing, and analyzing data

Determining and comparing averages

Overview

We encounter chance every day. Will it rain? Will our favorite team win? Will we be in an accident? Will our guess be correct? Is the game fair? Our language is rich with words and phrases for describing different levels of probability: *usually, sometimes, occasionally, rarely; a sure thing, as likely as not, a long shot, once in a blue moon,* and many other colorful expressions. In *Chance Encounters: Probability in Games and Simulations,* students learn to see probability through a mathematical lens by exploring and creating games and simulations and by applying the concept of probability to events from their own lives.

In the roles of games testers and designers, students conduct experiments with simple games and consider the probabilities of a number of everyday events. While doing so, they sharpen their intuitions and correct misconceptions about such concepts as randomness and luck. Throughout the unit, students learn new models for representing, comparing and analyzing probabilities: probability lines to rank the likelihood of different events; percentages, fractions, decimals, and ratios to quantify probabilities; area models, like circular spinners, to visualize probabilities; and grid models to depict all the possible outcomes.

All of these models help students make the transition from games players and testers to game designers. For example, students use the grid models and numerical representations to evaluate whether a game is fair or unfair and to determine how to change an unfair game to make it fair. In the process, they investigate the relationship of theoretical probabilities—those derived from logical analysis of all the possible outcomes—to experimental probabilities—those based on data from actual trials. Students apply this knowledge in the final section when they explore and evaluate simulations, comparing the probabilities in the simulation to data from the actual events. Finally, they use everything they have learned to create and test their own simulations.

Through these activities, students learn basic concepts of probability, such as natural variability and the law of large numbers. They learn the processes of conducting mathematical experiments, collecting and analyzing data, and developing logical arguments. They learn the mathematical underpinnings of simulations, which are becoming widely used in many fields. And, most important, they learn how mathematical thinking can provide insights into the world around them.

How This Unit Is Organized

Section 1 *Introduction to Chance*

In Section 1, students conduct probability experiments to analyze a variety of games played with coins and number cubes. They explore the variability of results in chance games by (1) gathering and comparing individual results and (2) comparing individual results with whole-class results. Students also describe and rank the likelihood of real-world events qualitatively (from never to always) and quantitatively (from 0 to 1 and from 0% to 100%).

Section 2 *Spinner Games: Multiple Representations of Probability*

In Section 2, students test and design games played with circular spinners, which provide a clear visual model of probability. Students predict the distribution of outcomes from spinners with unequal probabilities and test their predictions. They then draw spinners to match clues that describe probabilities in numbers and words. Students bring together visual, numeric, and verbal descriptions when they create clues and spinners for their own games.

Section 3 *Fair and Unfair Games*

Section 3 focuses on determining whether games are fair or unfair. Students test the fairness of games involving two independent events, such as the tossing of two number cubes. After making predictions and conducting experiments, students create an outcome grid that shows the theoretical probabilities of all the possible outcomes in the game. As students compare games played with different rules and game pieces, they explore the relationship between outcome grids, experimental data, and various numeric representations of probability.

Section 4 *Simulations: Using Probability to Model Real-World Events*

In Section 4, students analyze and create games that are designed to simulate real-world activities. Students conduct experiments to test the realism of the simulations, to see whether the probabilities of events in the simulations reflect the probabilities in the actual activity. After analyzing the results, students change the probabilities in the simulation to make it more realistic. This activity helps prepare students for the final project, in which they design their own simulation of an activity of their choice. The final project gives students the opportunity to apply and extend what they have learned in the unit.

Appendix A   *"Dear Dr. Math"*

In these writing activities, students play the role of a newspaper columnist answering questions about mathematics. These writing prompts can be used throughout the unit as discussion starters, homework, and assessment. The accompanying notes that describe the mathematics concepts involved in each problem can be used as assessment criteria.

Appendix B   *Sample Student Projects*

This appendix includes the final projects of students in classrooms in which this unit was field-tested.

Appendix C   *Reproducible Blackline Masters*

Whenever a lesson requires a reproducible, a master has been provided in both English and Spanish. Depending on the structure of your classroom, you may prefer to copy the master onto an overhead transparency to be used with the whole class.

Mathematical Themes in This Unit

Throughout *Chance Encounters: Probability in Games and Simulations,* students encounter three major mathematical themes, each briefly described below. The individual section overviews provide specific information about how these themes are addressed in the lessons in that section.

Theoretical and Experimental Probability

Mathematically speaking, a probability is a ratio that tells us how likely it is that something will occur. The probability of a tossed coin's landing on heads is 1:2; the probability of a tossed number cube's landing on 3 is 1:6. Probabilities range from 0 to 1; they can never be greater than one because it is impossible to have a ratio with more favorable events than possible events.

In this unit, students learn about two ways to determine probabilities. One is to analyze the situations and logically determine all the possible outcomes and the probability of each outcome. For example, we know that a coin can land on either heads or tails and there is an equal probability of each outcome. We can use this information to determine mathematically the probability of different outcomes with any number of coins: If we flip a coin twice (and keep track of the order in which heads and tails occur), there are four possible outcomes—HH, HT, TH, TT—each with a probability of 1:4. Probability determined by logical analysis is called *theoretical probability.*

In many situations, we cannot know all the possibilities and their probabilities. For example, suppose you toss a thumbtack instead of a coin. We know the thumbtack is not symmetrical, so it seems unlikely that point-up and point-down are equally likely, but we have no logical way of determining the exact likelihood of each outcome. The only way to find out would be to experiment. We could, for example, toss the thumbtack 100 times and count how often each outcome occurs. We then have *experimental probability*—probability based on data of what actually happened, rather than on a theoretical or logical analysis.

Throughout the unit, students collect probability data by doing experiments; playing games; and gathering data from existing sources, such as newspapers and almanacs. They record and organize their results and learn to represent data with tables, strip graphs, and bar graphs. They also work with statistical concepts, such as average and range, and make inferences and generalizations from their experimental results.

As students conduct experiments with coins, number cubes, and circular spinners, they compare their results with their classmates' results and with the theoretical probabilities of the situations. These comparisons help students gain a sense of the natural variability of results: When probability is involved, the outcome of each individual event is random, so it cannot be predicted in advance. Students also gain an intuitive sense of the law of large numbers: as the number of trials increases, the experimental results are likely to become closer to the theoretical probabilities. Students learn that they need to collect large amounts of data to draw reliable and accurate conclusions about probabilities.

This work with theoretical and experimental probability provides a solid foundation for studying probability and statistics in later grades.

Multiple Representations of Probability

Throughout the unit, students represent probability qualitatively, with words; visually, with several different models; and quantitatively, with percentages, fractions, and decimals.

Students develop lists of words and phrases that refer to different probabilities (*definitely, likely, not a chance,* etc.), and they share and compare their interpretations of these verbal descriptions. As students explore their own interpretations of words describing probabilities, they come to understand the need to develop more precise descriptions in mathematics.

Visual representations enable students to describe and compare probabilities in ways that are easy to understand. One visual representation shows probability as a number line. One end of the line represents *never;* the other end *always.* The midpoint represents a 50% probability. The probability of different events is shown by placing the events along the probability line. This representation is useful for estimating and comparing probabilities.

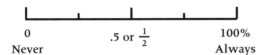

0	.5 or $\frac{1}{2}$	100%
Never		Always

Another visual representation uses the areas of parts on a circular spinner to represent probabilities. For example, the two spinners below represent the probability of each outcome when a coin is tossed and when a number cube is thrown. Area representations are useful for showing all the possible outcomes and the probability of each.

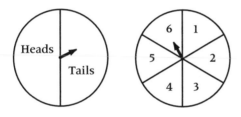

The outcome grid is used to show the possible outcomes and probabilities when two events, such as tossing two coins, are involved. The outcome grid below shows the possible four outcomes of tossing two coins.

Outcome Grid

Coin 1

Coin 2		H	T
	H	HH	TH
	T	HT	TT

Students relate these visual representations to three types of numeric representations of probabilities: percentages, fractions, and decimals. They discover the advantages of each representation (e.g., percentages make it easier to compare probabilities obtained from experiments with different numbers of trials—it is easier to compare 68% and 63% than it is to compare $^{17}/_{25}$ and $^{22}/_{35}$). Students learn that probabilities range from 0 to 1, and they learn to translate from one numeric form to another.

Modeling Situations with Simulations

One of the major applications of probability is to develop simulations of real-world situations. Students may be familiar with video games that simulate playing a sport, piloting an airplane, planning a city, etc. Simulations are widely used in many professions. Architects use them to test building designs, businesses use them to develop marketing plans, and scientists use them to develop and test hypotheses.

In this unit, students design and test their own simulations. They choose a topic or situation, analyze the events that could happen, and collect data about the probability of each possible event. The challenge is to design the simulation so that the probability of each simulated event mirrors the probability of the actual event. For example, in a baseball simulation, singles should be much more likely to occur than home runs. Students conduct experiments in which they test their simulations and compare the results to the real-world situations.

Letter to Families

A suggested letter to families describing the unit and suggesting activities that can be done at home is provided in both an English and a Spanish version. See Appendix C (Reproducible 1).

Lesson Schedule

The complete unit will require about 25 class periods, assuming class periods of at least 45 minutes. Pages xvii and xviii show a sample lesson-by-lesson schedule to help you plan.

Shorter Paths Through the Unit

This unit is designed so that all the lessons build and contribute to a whole that is greater than each part taken individually. For this reason, the ideal format is to use all the lessons. However, if you do not have enough time to do the whole unit, we recommend shortening the unit in one of two ways.

Approx. # of Classes	Lessons
Section 1: Introduction to Chance	
1	**1. Carnival Games** Students test a series of simple games involving coins and number cubes.
2	**2. Coins and Cubes: Predictions, Experiments, and Data** Students conduct experiments to investigate what might happen at multiple turns at one of the Carnival Games. They represent their results with strip graphs and frequency graphs to help build a picture of chance.
1	**3. From Never to Always: Describing the Likelihood of Events** Students use probability lines and qualitative descriptions to rank the likelihood of real-world events on a scale from *never* to *always*.
Section 2: Spinner Games: Multiple Representations of Probability	
1–2	**4. The Cover-Up Game** Students explore the probabilities in a game played with a circular spinner divided into unequal parts. They experiment with ways of changing the game to improve their chances of winning.
2	**5. Mystery Spinners** Students work in groups to design spinners to match a set of clues describing probabilities in words and numbers.
2	**6. Designing Mystery Spinner Games** Students design their own mystery spinner games. They exchange games with their classmates.

Approx. # of Classes	Lessons
Section 3: Fair and Unfair Games	
2	**7. Is It Fair?** Students test the fairness of a number-cube game. They use an outcome grid to show all the possible outcomes and determine each player's probability of getting points.
2	**8. Charting the Chances: Exploring Outcome Grids** Students make outcome grids to analyze a variety of fair and unfair games.
2	**9. Which Game Would You Play?** Students represent probabilities as fractions, decimals, percents, and ratios. They compare the probabilities of winning different unfair games.
Section 4: Simulations: Using Probability to Model Real-World Events	
2	**10. Is It Realistic? Testing Simulations** Students test simulation games that are played with a grid and two number cubes. They determine how realistic the games are by comparing data from playing the simulations with data from the actual sports.
2	**11. Simulating a Simple Game** Students collect data on a game of skill and then create a simulation to match their game results.
3+*	**12. Final Project: Design Your Own Simulation Game** Students design a simulation of an activity that they know well. They collect and analyze data, make a probability line, design an outcome-grid game board, and test their simulations.
1–2	**13. Project Seminar: Testing the Simulations** Students present their simulation games and play them.

*Time will vary depending on whether students work on the final project only during class or outside of class as well.

A: Cut the Simulation Investigations in Section 4

In the first three sections, students learn about theoretical and experimental probabilities and ways of representing them. They begin by experimenting and analyzing simple games and then move on to games that involve combinations of outcomes. This shortened version ends with students using different numeric and visual representations to compare the probabilities of winning unfair games. By cutting Section 4, students lose the opportunity to extend their knowledge by analyzing and designing simulations.

Section 1: As is.

Section 2: As is.

Section 3: As is.

Section 4: Cut.

Approximate time: 16 class periods.

B: Shorten the First Three Sections, But Keep Section 4

This option may be a good choice if your students have prior experience with probability. Students spend less time on the basic concepts in Section 1. In Section 2, they experiment with spinners, design spinners to match sets of clues describing probabilities in words and numbers, but skip creating their own clue games in Lesson 6. In Section 3, students determine whether games are fair or unfair by doing experiments and by finding theoretical probabilities but, by cutting Lesson 9, do not spend as much time comparing numerical representations of probabilities. In Section 4, students collect and analyze data for real-world events and then design simulations to reflect the probabilities of these events.

Section 1: Spend only one class period on Lesson 2.

Section 2: Skip Lesson 6.

Section 3: Skip Lesson 9.

Section 4: If students are comfortable with simulations after completing Lesson 10, then skip Lesson 11.

Approximate time: 20 class periods.

Preparing For and Teaching the Lessons

A brief overview at the beginning of each section describes how the major mathematical themes are dealt with in the section's lessons. Each section also contains one or two Teacher Reflections that describe directions a lesson took in an actual classroom and provide the teacher's analysis of students' thinking and learning in that lesson.

Each lesson contains the following features:

- A brief overview of the lesson's goals and activities.
- The materials needed for the lesson.
- A suggested lesson plan outlining steps you might use in teaching the lesson. Each step in a lesson is labeled to describe the general nature of the activity:

    Investigation denotes an open-ended and extended inquiry, with students determining their own approaches and finding their own solutions.

    Problem solving indicates a question with a somewhat smaller scope and more specific parameters, but one that still requires students to devise their own solutions.

    Discussion involves the whole class; *sharing* involves only a pair or small group of students.

    Practice is a task in which students apply a skill they have learned to a new situation.

- From the Classroom vignettes of suggestions and comments from teachers who have taught the unit, often including samples of their students' work. Some From the Classrooms are a composite of several teachers' experiences; others reflect what happened in one teacher's classroom.
- Homework Possibilities. These optional activities, provided at the end of the lesson plan, reinforce and extend the material covered in the lesson. They are never prerequisites for the next day or for subsequent lessons. Options are provided so that teachers can choose assignments that fit the needs of their students and their schools' homework policies.

    Some lessons also contain these features:

- To the Student boxes with information students need about a key activity in the lesson.
- Assessment Criteria to help you assess your students' work. See Assessing Students' Progress on page xxiii for more information on assessment.

- Answer keys for questions and student activities requiring answers that may not be self-evident.
- Extensions that provide additional challenges at various levels of difficulty.

Chance Encounters **Software**

A computer program is available to extend students' opportunities to explore and learn about probability. The program enables students to conduct experiments on the computer with simulated coins, number cubes, and spinners. Using the computer has three primary advantages:

1. Students can collect a large amount of data in a fraction of the time it would take to flip coins or spin spinners by hand. They can therefore explore patterns of results with more trials and rapidly conduct repeated experiments to see how the results vary.
2. Students can create their own spinners with unequal parts (or simulate weighted coins or cubes) and define the probability of each part. This feature enables students to change the theoretical probabilities of events easily and to conduct experiments to explore the effects of those changes.
3. Students can display the results as percentages, pie charts, and bar graphs as well as counts and can therefore easily produce and compare multiple representations of their data.

The program contains three different "labs." Activities provided with the software describe investigations and experiments that can be performed in each lab.

1. In the Game Piece Lab, students conduct experiments with coins, number cubes, and spinners similar to those in Section 1. Students can use this lab to design their own experiments throughout the unit.

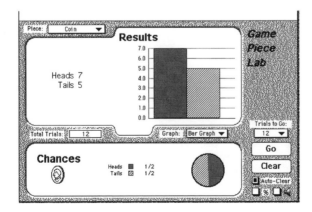

2. The Cover-Up Game Lab is designed to be used along with Section 2. The software contains various spinners, like those in the unit, and enables students to explore what happens when the Cover-Up game (from Lesson 4) is played with different strategies. Students can also create their own spinners for games, and explore the variability of results when a game is played multiple times.

3. The Game Fairness Lab is designed to be used along with Section 3. Students run experiments and analyze the results to determine whether the games are fair or unfair. In the unit, students revise the rules of games to make them fair. The software provides an alternative approach: students revise the spinners while keeping the rules the same.

The *Chance Encounters* software is designed to be used in three ways:

1. As a classroom demonstration tool, with one computer and a large screen in the classroom. This is particularly useful for encouraging discussion and comparing students' experimental data to simulated experiments with larger quantities of data.

2. At computer work stations within the classroom. Students take turns using the computer and are engaged in productive related activities when they are not at the computer.

3. In a computer lab, in which students, ideally working in pairs, all conduct experiments and investigations at the same time.

Materials to Obtain

The materials required for the unit are listed below. The reproducible masters for each lesson are listed at the beginning of the lesson.

Materials	*Amount*
Number cubes (in two different colors)	Two per pair (one cube of each color)
Transparent spinners*	One per pair
Coins or two-sided chips	One per pair
Tape	About four rolls per class
Markers or crayons (preferably the same color for the whole class)	One per pair
Inexpensive 4-function calculator	One per pair

Optional Materials

Overhead projector

Transparency markers

Chart paper

Ten-sided dice

Index cards for making digit cards (number the cards 0–9)

Three-ring binders or manila folders for storage of student work

Assessing Students' Progress

Middle school mathematics teachers today are using many assessment techniques. In addition to quizzes and tests, these include embedded assessment problems, projects, portfolios, and student self-assessments. This unit provides opportunities and support for a range of techniques. You may decide to use all or

Transparent spinners, which can be ordered from most educational supply catalogs, can be used for a variety of games by taping them to different spinner templates. These spinners also tend to be more reliable and sturdier than handmade options. As a lower-cost alternative, it is possible to construct temporary spinners using paper clips and pencils or pens. See Lesson 4 for more information on making spinners.

some of the opportunities listed below, or you may devise your own assessment methods.

Type of Assessment	Location
Embedded Assessment	Lesson 2
	Lesson 5
	Lesson 6
	Lesson 8
"Dr. Math" Problems	Available throughout the unit
Student Self-Assessment	Lesson 6
	Lesson 13
Final Project Assessment	Lesson 12

In many of the lessons, activities are identified as possibilities for embedded assessments. For example, the activities in which students improve flawed games and complete unfinished reports on experiments provide opportunities for them to demonstrate and apply what they know and can do. Most important, all of the assessment activities provide students with an opportunity to learn. In these ways, the assessment activities maintain rather than interrupt the flow of the unit. Assessment criteria are included to help you gather information for two purposes: to inform daily instructional decisions and to help you monitor students' individual growth over the course of the unit.

The "Dear Dr. Math" problems (Appendix A) provide opportunities for students to synthesize and communicate about the mathematics they are learning. Students take on the role of advice columnists and write letters to answer questions about probability and statistics. The writing process helps students synthesize content in the unit. These problems can be used throughout the unit as preassessments or assessments. A list of key points is provided for evaluating students' work.

The unit also includes questions for student self-assessment. Having students evaluate and write about their work encourages them to reflect on both the progress they've made and the relationship between product and process. As they explore this connection, students think about how they might improve their methods in the future.

Overall learning for the unit is assessed by way of a final project (Lesson 12) in which students design their own simulations. They collect data on real-world events, analyze the probabilities, design a game to simulate the probabilities, and write about the decisions they've made. The project is an open-ended assignment that provides students with a creative, authentic application of the mathematical knowledge they have gained in the unit. The lesson plan includes suggested assessment criteria to aid in evaluating student work on this project. Alternatively, the suggested criteria may be used as a starting point for the class to develop its own quality criteria.

Portfolios are particularly well suited to students' role as game designers in the unit. The games and simulations students create and revise make excellent portfolio material. Students select work from throughout the unit to include in their portfolios and write about: (1) why they selected each piece of work; (2) what they learned from each task; and (3) how they could improve their work. This process helps students communicate about the mathematics they have learned and helps them evaluate their own work. Reviewing the portfolios will help you assess students' progress on both specific and global mathematics goals.

Sources of Further Information

Books on Games

BELL, ROBBIE, AND MICHAEL CORNELIUS. *Board Games Around the World: A Resource Book for Mathematical Investigations.* Cambridge: Cambridge University Press, 1988.

BOTERMANS, JACK, TONY BURRETT, PIETER VAN DELFT, AND CARLA VAN SPLUNTEREN. *The World of Games.* New York: Facts on File, 1989.

COSTELLO, MATTHEW J. *The Greatest Games of All Time.* New York: John Wiley, 1991.

GRUNFELD, FREDERIC V., ED. *Games of the World.* New York: Ballantine, 1975.

Books on Teaching Probability and Statistics

LOVITT, CHARLES, AND IAN LOWE. *Chance and Data Investigations,* 2 vols. Portsmouth: Heinemann, 1994.

SHULTE, ALBERT P., AND JAMES R. SMART, EDS. *Teaching Statistics and Probability: 1981 Yearbook.* Reston, Virginia: National Council of Teachers of Mathematics, 1981.

ZAWOJEWSKI, JUDITH S. Dealing with Data and Chance. Curriculum and Evaluation Standards for School Mathematics Addenda Series, Grades 5–8. Reston, Virginia: National Council of Teachers of Mathematics, 1991.

Section 1

Introduction to Chance

In this section, students explore the concept of chance through a series of comparisons involving simple games. Students begin by playing a variety of games with coins and number cubes. As they compare their individual results for a small number of trials with the whole-class results, students build an understanding of randomness and natural variability. They also conduct probability experiments related to the games and compare how different graphical representations give different pictures of the results. In the final activity, students apply their growing knowledge of chance to describing and ranking the likelihood of real-world events.

The Game Piece Lab in the optional *Chance Encounters* software allows students to set up and run probability experiments on the computer. This enables them to collect large amounts of data quickly. An initial activity provided with the software introduces the process of running computer experiments. Other activities provide explorations involving natural variability, the law of large numbers, and the distinction between experimental and theoretical probability.

Approx. # of Classes	Lessons
1	**1. Carnival Games** Students test a series of simple games involving coins and number cubes.
2	**2. Coins and Cubes: Predictions, Experiments, and Data** Students conduct experiments to investigate what might happen at multiple turns at one of the Carnival Games. They represent their results with strip graphs and frequency graphs to help build a picture of chance.
1	**3. From Never to Always: Describing the Likelihood of Events** Students use probability lines and qualitative descriptions to rank the likelihood of real-world events on a scale from *never* to *always*.

Lesson summary and sample schedule for Section 1

Mathematical Themes

Theoretical and Experimental Probability

- Refine understanding of the concept of chance.
- Conduct probability experiments, including collecting, representing, and analyzing data.
- Develop an intuitive sense of natural variability: in a small number of trials the experimental results may be very different than the theoretical probabilities.
- Develop an intuitive sense of the law of large numbers: the larger the number of trials, the closer the outcomes get to the theoretical distribution.

This section introduces both the concept of probability and a process for exploring the concept through experimentation. As students begin to explore the games in Lesson 1, they consider the ratio of the number of wins to the number of attempts, which is the basic ratio concept of probability. Students refine their understanding of chance by collecting and analyzing data on a series of games played with coins and number cubes.

At key stages of the data collection process, students pause to investigate essential questions of probability: Which game rules give you a better chance of winning? Why do two students playing the same game get different results? Why might 10 turns at the game yield a different pattern of results from 100 turns? Questions like these lead students to consider the principle underlying the concept of natural variability and the law of large numbers: When probability is involved, you cannot accurately predict the outcome of individual trials, but you can predict the approximate number of each outcome over many trials.

Multiple Representations of Probability

- Represent data from experiments in different ways (with strip graphs, frequency graphs, and ratios, for example).
- Describe probabilities with qualitative terms (e.g., *likely, unlikely, always*).
- Describe probabilities quantitatively with decimals, fractions, percents, and ratios.
- Use a probability line to represent and compare the likelihood of events.

As students explore the games in Lesson 1, they find their own ways of describing probability and of comparing the chances of winning the games. Later in the section, students are introduced to specific ways to represent probabilities.

In Lesson 2, students represent the results of their experiments with strip graphs. A strip graph is a series of boxes, each representing one trial in the experiment. The box is filled with a color or pattern representing the outcome of that trial.

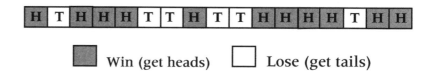

■ Win (get heads)   □ Lose (get tails)

Since strip graphs show the sequence of outcomes, they provide a strong picture of the variability of results. Students see not only that the number of wins in 20 turns at the same game can be quite different for different students, but also that the order of wins can be different: one student may win five times in a row, while another might win on every other toss or in no particular pattern.

While strip graphs are useful for highlighting the variability of results, they are cumbersome for analyzing large numbers of trials. To consider the data for the entire class, students create frequency graphs, from which they get a sense of which results are typical and which are unlikely and therefore develop an intuitive sense of the law of large numbers.

What might happen in 20 turns at the Get Ahead Booth?

X = 1 Pair of
Students

```
          X X X   X
          X X X X X X X
      X   X X X X X X X
  ─────────────────────────────────────────
  1  2  3  4  5  6  7  8  9 10 11 12 13 14 15 16 17 18 19 20
```

Number of Heads Each Pair Got in 20 Coin Tosses

In Lesson 3, students explore connections among visual and numerical representations as they describe the likelihood of real-world events. Students use probability lines and qualitative descriptions (*never, likely, always*) to describe and rank the likelihood of different events happening on a typical school day. They then add percentage, fraction, and decimal scales to the probability line, thereby relating the numeric and visual representations.

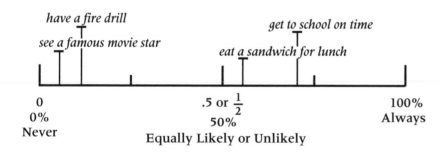

have a fire drill

see a famous movie star

get to school on time

eat a sandwich for lunch

0
0%
Never

.5 or $\frac{1}{2}$
50%

Equally Likely or Unlikely

100%
Always

Modeling Situations with Simulations

• Rank the probabilities of events on a scale of 0 to 1.

In this section, students begin describing and comparing the probabilities of real-world events. They choose an activity that they know well, such as going to school or playing a sport. Students list events that are part of the activity and rank them from least likely to most likely to occur on a probability line. This helps prepare students for the first steps of designing simulations (in Section 4): analyzing and comparing the probabilities of the events to be simulated.

In the first class, I began with a discussion of What is chance? Several students defined chance in terms of luck.

"[Probability is] the luck of getting something."

"Everything's luck, you don't know when you'll get a 3 or a 6 [when you roll a number cube]."

"Just because you are better it doesn't necessarily mean you'll win. There's always luck. You never know."

As the discussion progressed, I became aware of several misconceptions that students had about probability. Sonia insisted that she could increase her chances of rolling a three by practicing. She thought that if she went home and practiced rolling a number cube she would be able to make it land on the number she wanted. Many of her classmates challenged her to try it. Some students felt that everything has a 50-50 chance, no matter what.

"In basketball there is a 50-50 chance of getting a basket. You either get it in or you miss."

"Everything in baseball is a 50-50 chance. I have a 50-50 chance of striking out and a 50-50 chance of getting on base."

When I introduced the rules of the Carnival Games, several students predicted they would win a large number of tickets because they thought they were "lucky." Dan said that the probability of winning tickets at the Pick a Number booth was low, but he still thought he'd win a lot because he's lucky. In contrast, Miguel thought he would do badly because he always loses at games. Students' perceptions of themselves as "lucky" or "unlucky" seemed to color their predictions of how they would do in the game.

I was struck by the conviction with which students voiced their misconceptions, and I realized that I wouldn't be able to change their minds by just talking to them about it. I found it was helpful for students to have the concrete experiences of doing the coin and number-cube experiments in Lesson 2. In the class discussion, I focused on the contrast between students' individual results and the results of the class as a whole. Students could see that making generalizations based on an individual's results could be unreliable. By the end of the lesson, I felt I had made a good start at addressing students' misconceptions.

LUCKY 3s
BOOTH

GET AHEAD
BOOTH

Tickets

Heads = 1 Ticket
Tails = 0

Lesson 1

Carnival Games

What is chance? How can an understanding of chance help you when you play a game?

In this lesson, students begin their role as game designers by testing a collection of games of chance presented in the context of carnival booths. Each game involves tossing coins or number cubes and each has different rules for winning "prize tickets." Students choose which games to play and then compare their individual experiences with the pattern of results for the whole class. The comparison gives students a sense of the variability of results in games of chance. The comparison also encourages students to think about the relationship between chance and choice: since the probabilities of the games differ, which booths they choose will influence the number of tickets they win.

In Lesson 2, students will conduct experiments to find out more about the probabilities of the different carnival games.

Mathematical Goals

- Refine understanding of the concept of chance.
- Explore the variability of results in games of chance.

Materials

Per Student

Reproducible 1, *Letter to Families* (optional)

Reproducible 4, *Improving the Carnival Games*

Per Pair

Reproducible 2, *Carnival Games*

Reproducible 3, *Carnival Games Scoresheet*

1 number cube

1 coin

Preparation

Reproducible 1

You may want to hand out the *Letter to Families* (Reproducible 1), which provides a description of the unit and the mathematics involved.

Suggested Lesson Plan

1. Introduction: *What is chance? What real-world experiences involve chance?*

Students discuss their understanding of the concept of chance and situations in which they encounter chance in their everyday lives. Some sample questions include:

- What is chance? Give some examples of situations that involve chance.
- What games do you play that involve chance? Do all games involve chance?
- What games do you play that involve things other than chance, such as making choices or using physical skills?
- How do carnivals and fairs involve chance?

▶ **From the Classroom**

For definitions of chance, students suggested things like "luck," "when you don't know," and "50-50." There was some confusion because chance also means an opportunity to do something. As examples of situations where chance plays a role, students came up with the weather, lotteries, and sports.

▶ *I started out the lesson by asking students about their experiences at carnivals and fairs. Most students had either been to one or seen one in a television show or video. Students gave differing opinions on the chances of winning a prize at a carnival booth. Most thought winning a prize was very unlikely. "You have a one in a zillion chance of getting a prize." "I think those booths are rigged so you can't get a prize."*

2. Investigation: *Test the carnival games.*

The following memo introduces students' role as apprentice game designers. Part of that role involves testing and analyzing new games—like the ones in this lesson. As students examine a variety of games, they think about the qualities and features they want to include or avoid in their own designs.

MEMO 1

To: Apprentice Game Designers
From: Company Directors

Welcome to AllPlay. We've got lots of work for you to do. You'll be trying out new games, analyzing them, improving them, and creating your own. To help you design games that are fair and fun to play, you'll be learning about probability and statistics.

Your first assignment is to work on a new collection of games called Carnival Games. We've made a rough draft of the board and now it's time to test it. It's hard to tell how good a game is from just one person's experience. One player could do great while another does terribly. That's why we want all of you to try the games and tell us what you think. We want your ideas on how to improve these games.

Introduce the *Carnival Games* (Reproducible 2) to your students by playing a few turns at a couple of different booths. Students win tickets at the booths in different ways, such as getting heads or rolling an even number. Students choose which games to play. In a later step, they will write about the chances of winning at different booths. Students record their results on the *Carnival Games Scoresheet* (Reproducible 3); this data will be used in the next step.

The games are played in pairs. (For a group of three, an additional scoresheet is needed.) Each student gets ten turns; a turn is one time at a game. Background information on the probabilities in the games is provided at the end of the lesson.

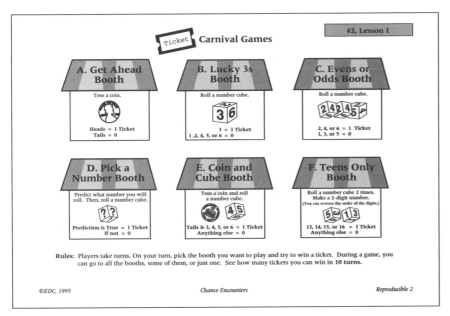

Reproducible 2

3. Discussion: *Compare the number of tickets you won to the number your classmates won.*

Create a class chart or graph showing the total number of tickets each student won. (The data for all the games is combined because there will not be enough data on any one game to make accurate comparisons.) As students compare their scores with their classmates' data, they get a sense of the variability of results. The differences in students' experiences are due in part to chance and, in part, to the choices students made. The results from one classroom are shown on page 12.

Number of Tickets Each Student Won

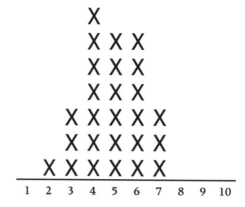

X represents one student

At this early stage of the unit, the discussion questions should focus on students' experiences playing the games rather than on any formal, numerical representation of probabilities. For example:

- How did your results compare with the results of the whole class?
- Which booths did you go to? Why?
- Are you more likely to win a ticket or not win a ticket on a turn?
- What would you do differently if you played again?

4. Writing: *Which booth gives you the best chance of winning tickets?*

As students compare the chances of winning at the different booths, they explore probability concepts in an informal way. Since this is the first lesson in the unit, students are not expected to know all the answers, but their responses can provide you with information about their prior knowledge of probability.

TO THE STUDENT

1. Pick two booths to compare. Are players more likely to win tickets at one of the booths? Why or why not?
2. Design a strategy that would give players a good chance of winning tickets.
   a. Which booths would you go to? Why?
   b. How many tickets do you think a player would be likely to win in 10 turns if he or she played with your strategy? Why?
   c. How many tickets do you think a player would be likely to win in 100 turns if he or she played with your strategy? Why?

► **From the Classroom**

Some students gave a surprising answer for question 2c. For example, one student won 7 tickets in 10 turns and then predicted he would win 97 tickets in 100 turns. He figured in both cases he would win zero tickets on three turns. This let me know that I would need to focus on developing proportional reasoning throughout the unit.

► a. Which booths would you go to? Why?

I would go to Get Ahead Booth, Evens or Odds booth, and Heads or Tails Booth because you have a better chance of winning. It's either get what you're supposed to or you don't; You have a fifty fifty chance.

b. How many tickets do you think you would win in 10 turns when you play with your new strategy? Why?

I think I would win about 4 tickets if I played with my new strategy, because you have a fifty fifty chance. Since you only have a fifty fifty chance you don't have a very good chance of getting a ticket every time. You can't be too optimistic. Fifty fifty chance is like saying you might get 5 tickets if you play 10 times.

c. How many tickets do you think you would win in 100 turns if you played with your new strategy? Why?

I think I would win about 50 tickets if I played with my new strategy because when you hav more turns it seems like there's a better chance for you to win.

5. Problem Solving: *Design new booths for the Carnival Games.*

Improving the Carnival Games (Reproducible 4) asks students to revise some of the games or create new ones. This activity works well for homework.

► *From the Classroom*

Students came up with creative ideas for new booths—for example, "Age Booth: If you can roll the dice twice in a row so that it will say the first and last digit of your age, you win 3 tickets." Some changed the scoring system so that players could win many more tickets on each turn. Other students added places where players could double their winnings or lose all of them.

► *One of my students explained that he decided to make the Lucky 3s booth better by giving the player "a 3 out of 4 chance." He decided the booth would use a 4-sided die and if the player rolled a 1, 2, or 4 then he or she would get tickets. I asked him if that was better for the booth owner and he explained that "it's a kid's fair and little kids should have a better chance of winning."*

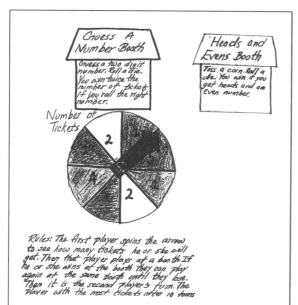

a) How could you change a booth or design a new one to give players a __better__ chance of winning tickets?

IF I could change a booth I would change the Lucky 3s booth because it was really hard. I would make it so you won 5 ticket instead of 1.

b) How could you change a booth or design a new one to give players a __worse__ chance of winning tickets?

To give players a worse chances of winning make the even number's booth just number 2.

Homework Possibilities

Problem Solving

Improving the Carnival Games (Reproducible 4) works well as homework.

Data Collection

Students play the Carnival Games with friends or family members. They compare the results to what happened in class and interview people to find out what games they like to play and why. They also interview them about their experiences at carnivals and fairs. Do they like games that involve chance? Have they won prizes at carnival booths? What do they think the chances are of winning a prize?

Background Information on Carnival Games Probabilities

The Carnival Games give students the opportunity to have concrete experiences with coins and number cubes and to begin articulating their ideas about probability. Since this is the first lesson, students will discuss probabilities in an informal or qualitative manner. They are not expected to use numerical representations or to come up with all the information described below.

The Get Ahead and Evens or Odds booths give students a .5 or 50% chance of winning. In the Get Ahead booth, students have 1 way of winning out of the 2 ways the coin can land. In the Evens or Odds booth, students have 3 ways of winning out of the 6 ways the cube can land.

The Lucky 3s and Pick a Number booths give students a 1 in 6 chance of winning tickets. Some students may think that these booths have different probabilities because one involves making predictions. They may think that their lucky number has a better than 1 in 6 chance of coming up when they roll a number cube.

The remaining two booths are more complicated, because they involve two tosses of the game pieces.

The Coin and Cube booth gives students a 1 in 3 chance of winning. There are 12 possible outcomes when you toss a coin and number cube (6 number cube outcomes multiplied by 2 coin outcomes.) There are four ways to win: T3, T4, T5, and T6.

The Teens Only booth gives students an 8 in 36 or 22% probability of winning. There are 36 possible combinations when you roll a number cube twice (6 outcomes on the first roll multiplied by 6 outcomes on the second roll). There are 8 ways of rolling the winning numbers: 13, 31, 14, 41, 15, 51, 16, and 61.

The following table provides information for comparing the different booths:

Booth	Number of Ways of Winning	Number of Possible Outcomes	Theoretical Probability of Winning	Expected Number of Wins in 10 Turns
A. Get Ahead	1	2	$\frac{1}{2}$ or .5	5
B. Lucky 3s	1	6	$\frac{1}{6}$ or .167	1.67
C. Evens or Odds	3	6	$\frac{3}{6}$ or .5	5
D. Pick a Number	1	6	$\frac{1}{6}$ or .167	1.67
E. Coin and Cube	4	12	$\frac{4}{12}$ or .33	3.3
F. Teens Only	8	36	$\frac{8}{36}$ or .22	2.2

Lesson 2

Coins or Cubes: Predictions, Experiments, and Data

How can you do an experiment to find out more about your chances of winning a game? If everyone in the class does the same experiment, will everyone get the same results?

In this lesson, students conduct an experiment to investigate what might happen in multiple turns at one of the Carnival Game booths. Students make predictions and then gather data on 20 turns at one of the booths. They learn to record their data on a strip graph, which provides a strong visual model of the variability of results. After comparing strip graphs, students use them to create a frequency graph showing whole-class results. In the process, students come to recognize the importance of having a lot of data instead of relying on a small number of trials. They also learn a method for conducting probability experiments that they will use throughout the unit. The lesson ends with an assessment of what students have learned in Lessons 1 and 2.

Mathematical Goals

- Conduct probability experiments.
- Build an intuitive sense of natural variability: in a small number of trials the experimental results may be very different from the theoretical probabilities.
- Build an intuitive sense of the law of large numbers: the larger the number of trials, the closer the outcomes are likely to get to the theoretical distribution.
- Represent data from experiments in different ways, for example with strip graphs, frequency graphs, and ratios.

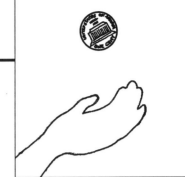

Materials

Per Student

Reproducible 6, *What Might Happen?*

Reproducible 7, *Unfinished Report*

Calculator (optional)

Per Pair

Reproducible 2, *Carnival Games*

Reproducible 5, *Strip Graph Templates*

Graph Paper

Crayons or markers

Coin

Number cube

Per Class

Chart paper, for making graphs

Tape

Preparation

Reproducible 5

Copy and cut the *Strip Graph Templates* (Reproducible 5) so that there are 2 strips of 10 boxes each per pair of students. The two strips should be taped together to make one long strip of 20 boxes.

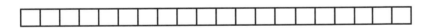

Suggested Lesson Plan

1. Writing: *What might happen in 20 turns at one of the carnival game booths?*

This activity is designed to get students thinking about the variability of results that might occur in 20 turns at a booth.

TO THE STUDENT

Two students are having a conversation about their experiences at a carnival:

Andre: "I lucked out. I was doing so well that I stayed at the same booth the whole time. I won 15 times out of 20. I don't know how that booth stays in business."

Kim: "That's not what happened to me. When I started out, I lost 3 times in a row. I stayed at the same booth because I thought things had to get better. But they didn't. I only won 8 times out of 20. I think that booth is a rip-off."

Write answers to these questions about the conversation:

- Is it possible that Kim and Andre went to the same booth? Why or why not?

- Which of the carnival game booths do you think Andre and Kim went to? Why?

Reproducible 6

▶ **From the Classroom**

My students had a lot of experience with coin tossing, so I chose to do a number-cube experiment. I thought that an experiment on the Lucky 3s booth might present the most surprises. Many people think that 3 is indeed a "lucky" number. I wanted students to look at the results to see if 3 was luckier than the other numbers. I expected they would find that different numbers would come up more frequently for different pairs of students and that no one number was "lucky" for the whole class.

2. Investigation: *Conduct an experiment on one of the carnival game booths.*

What Might Happen (Reproducible 6) guides students through the process of making predictions, gathering data, and representing the results for a probability experiment. Choose booth A, B, or C for the class to test and then have students write answers to questions 1–3 on the handout. It's important for the whole class to test the same game so that you will have a large number of trials to compile and analyze.

The Get Ahead, Lucky 3s, and Evens and Odds booths work well for this first experiment and provide a good foundation for analyzing the other booths. The Coin and Cube and Teens Only booths are more complex because they involve outcomes that are combinations from two tosses of coins or number cubes. These kinds of combinations will be addressed in Section 3.

While some students will figure out the theoretical probabilities of winning at booths A, B and C, they may not have a sense of how these probabilities will play out in an experiment. For example, the probability of getting heads is 50%; does that mean that every other toss will land on heads? The goal of the experiments is to give students a sense of the variability of results when working with chance.

**What Might Happen in 20 Turns
at One of the Carnival Booths?**

1. **Make predictions.**

• How many wins do you think you will get in 20 turns? ☐

• What do you think the highest number of wins in the class will be? ☐

The lowest? ☐

• What do you think the most common number of wins will be? ☐

2. **Conduct the experiment and record your results.**

With a partner, take turns tossing a coin or number cube. Record the results on a strip graph, like the ones below. Before each toss, predict what you will get. When you are done, color in the boxes where you would win tickets.

Sample Strip Graphs:

Get Ahead Booth | H | H | T | H | T | H | H | T | H | T | H | H | H | H | H | H | T |

☐ Win   ☐ Lose (0 Tickets)

Evens or Odds Booth | 2 | 3 | 5 | 4 | 4 | 6 | 1 | 2 | 5 | 4 | 1 | 3 | 2 | 5 | 6 | 6 |

Lucky 3's Booth | 2 | 3 | 5 | 4 | 4 | 6 | 1 | 2 | 5 | 4 | 1 | 3 | 2 | 5 | 3 | 6 | 5 | 4 |

	Your Results	Class Results
Total number of wins		
Longest number of wins in a row		
Highest number of wins in class		
Lowest number of wins in class		
Most common number of wins(mode)		

Reproducible 6

3. Data collection: *Record your results as a strip graph.*

Students use the strip graph templates to record their results. Unlike many other types of graphs, strip graphs show the sequence of outcomes, which helps to highlight the differences among individual results and provides a strong visual representation of the concept of randomness. After completing 20 trials, students color all the boxes that show "wins" (turns for which they would win tickets). Having all the students use the same color (e.g., red) makes the graphs easier to compare.

Get Ahead Booth
| H | H | T | H | T | H | H | H | T | H | T | H | H | H | H | H | H | H | T | T | H | T |

☐ Win   ☐ Lose (0 Tickets)

Evens and Odds Booth
| 2 | 3 | 5 | 4 | 4 | 6 | 1 | 2 | 5 | 4 | 1 | 3 | 2 | 5 | 6 | 6 | 5 | 4 | 1 | 5 |

Lucky 3's Booth
| 2 | 3 | 5 | 4 | 4 | 6 | 1 | 2 | 5 | 4 | 1 | 3 | 2 | 5 | 3 | 6 | 5 | 4 | 1 | 5 |

▶ **From the Classroom**

I had students make predictions before each toss. This added an element of fun to the testing and gave them a sense of the unpredictability of events involving chance.

4. Discussion: *How do your results compare with your classmates' results?*

Put the strip graphs together to make a large class chart to facilitate the comparison of results. Here are 5 of the 16 strip graphs in a class chart for the Get Ahead booth.

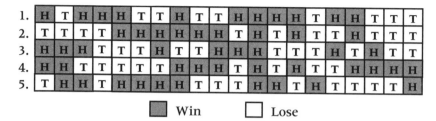

| | Win | | Lose |

The focus of this discussion is on exploring the visual model of variability provided by the strip graphs. After students make frequency graphs in Step 5, they will be ready to calculate the total number of wins and losses.

- How does your strip graph compare with your classmates'?
- Do any of the strip graphs look the same?
- What is the longest number of wins in a row? losses in a row?
- Without counting the total number of wins and losses for the class, look at all the strip graphs to see how the colors compare. Does one color seem to come up more than the other or do they look about the same?

5. Problem Solving: *What would a frequency graph show us about our results?*

Make a class frequency graph of the number of wins each pair of students got. While strip graphs highlight the differences among the results, frequency graphs show the similarities. Students can see quickly which number of wins is typical and which is unusual. Some questions for analyzing the results include:

- What is the most common number of wins? the highest? the lowest?
- What does the distribution of wins look like? Are there any clumps? Is it spread out?
- How do the results compare with your predictions?
- How do Kim's and Andre's results compare with the class results? How likely is it that they went to the same booth used in the experiment?
- How does the frequency graph compare with the strip graph?

From the Classroom

Posting the strip graphs really helped my students see the idea of randomness. One student, who got 5 heads in a row, announced, "Oh my gosh, look what I got!" when he saw his strip graph among the others.

Initially, I wasn't sure what to do about our unusual class results for the Get Ahead booth: most students got more than 10 heads. There was a lot of discussion about whether heads was really more likely, with students citing past experiences to support or challenge the idea. The discussion motivated students to repeat the experiment to see what would happen. In the end, I felt the unusual results stimulated a lot of learning that the expected results might not have.

What might happen in 20 turns at the Get Ahead Booth?

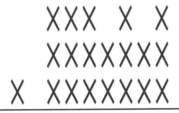

```
XXX  X  X
XXXXXXX
X XXXXXXX
─────────────────────────────────
1  2  3  4  5  6  7  8  9  10 11 12 13 14 15 16 17 18 19 20
```

Number of Wins (Heads)

X = one pair of students
(20 pairs in the class)

6. **Problem Solving:** *How does the total number of wins compare with the total number of tosses? How do your individual results compare with the class results?*

TO THE STUDENT

Use the class frequency graph to calculate:
- The total number of wins.
- The total number of losses.
- The total number of tosses.
- What percentage of the total number of tosses in the class were wins? That's called the *experimental probability* for getting a win.
- What percentage of your tosses were wins?

The ratio of wins to tosses is called the experimental probability of wins. The experimental probability of the whole-class results is likely to be closer to the theoretical probability than that of the students' individual results. After students have completed their calculations, encourage the class to reflect on the results with questions such as:

- How do your individual results compare to the class results?
- If you did 1,000 tosses, how many wins do you think you would get? Why?

7. Assessment: *Finish a report on an experiment.*

Unfinished Report (Reproducible 7) provides data from an experiment that involves 40 tosses of a number cube. Students organize and analyze the results and describe the experimental probabilities of the number cube landing on an odd or an even number.

Homework Possibilities

Writing

Dr. Math letters A–D (Appendix A).

Problem Solving

- *Unfinished Report* (Reproducible 7) works well as homework.
- Students use the class frequency graph from Step 5 to help plan a school fair.

TO THE STUDENT

The planning committee wants to know what you think of their ideas for the school fair. They are planning to have a booth just like the one in your experiment. Each student will get 20 turns at the booth. Students will get prizes depending on how many wins they get.

School Fair Prizes	Number of Wins Needed
Lemonade	0–4 wins
Ice cream	5–9 wins
Small stuffed animal	exactly 10 wins
T-shirt	11–15 wins
Giant stuffed animal	16–20 wins

Answer these question using your class frequency graph:

1. Based on the frequency graph from your class experiment, which prizes do you think the planning committee should buy the most of? why? the least of? why?

2. Based on your frequency graph, what percentage of the pairs of students in the class would get each prize?

3. Pick a prize that you like. How would you change the number of wins so that about 50% of the students would get that prize?

Investigation

Students design a game piece using common materials (such as beans, popsicle sticks, and tape) and then conduct an experiment to determine the probabilities of its landing on each of its sides. Unlike coins and number cubes, the student-made piece will probably be asymmetrical and so the probabilities of its landing on each of its sides will be different. Students have made game pieces with bottle caps filled with beans and covered with tape or with "casting sticks" made from popsicle sticks and straws. (Casting sticks are used in the ancient Egyptian game *Senet.*)

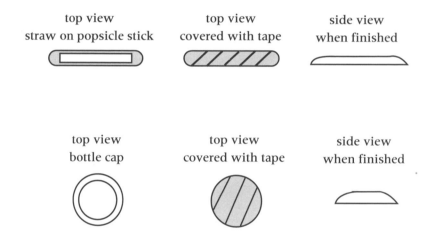

| top view
straw on popsicle stick | top view
covered with tape | side view
when finished |
| top view
bottle cap | top view
covered with tape | side view
when finished |

Software Possibilities

With the *Chance Encounters* software program, students can easily simulate running coin and number-cube experiments with large numbers of trials, such as 1,000 tosses. In addition, they can run a series of experiments with the same number of trials (such as 10 experiments with 20 tosses each) and compare the results. These types of activities provide excellent extensions to the investigation in this lesson.

Answers to *Unfinished Report* (Reproducible 7)

1. At right is a sample bar graph of data from the experiment.
2. The experimental probabilities are:

   Odd Numbers: $^{24}/_{40}$ or 60%

   Even Numbers: $^{16}/_{40}$ or 40%
3. In 1,000 trials, you would expect the results to be closer to the theoretical probabilities; you might get about 500 odd numbers and 500 even numbers.
4. Since the theoretical probability of getting an even number is 50%, it would take about 160 tosses to get 80 even numbers. If you base the estimate on the experimental probability (40%), it would take about 200 tosses.

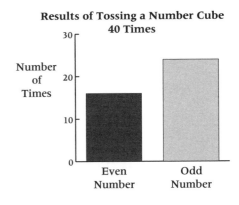

Results of Tossing a Number Cube 40 Times

Answers to Homework
Problem Solving: School Fair

Answers will vary depending on the class results for the experiment. Answers for the Get Ahead Booth and Evens and Odds booth may be similar to the example below. However, those for the Lucky 3s booth are likely to be quite different because the probability of winning is $^1/_6$ instead of $^1/_2$.

The following answers are for the sample graph at right. This graph has been divided to show how many pairs of students will win each prize.

1. For sample graph: The planning committee should buy the most ice cream and T-shirts and the least lemonade and giant stuffed animals.
2. For sample graph:

   Lemonade: 0%

   Ice Cream: $^{10}/_{20}$ or 50%

   Small Stuffed Animal: $^2/_{20}$ or 10%

   T-Shirt: $^8/_{20}$ or 40%

   Giant Stuffed Animal: 0%
3. For sample graph: if you change the number of wins to the following, then 10 of the 20 pairs or 50% will win that prize.

   Giant Stuffed Animal: 9–12 wins

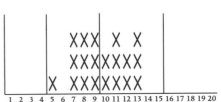

What might happen in 20 turns at the Get Ahead Booth?

Number of Wins (Heads)

X = one pair of students
(20 pairs in the class)

From Never to Always: Describing the Likelihood of Events

1 in a million (?)

How can you describe the probability of real-world events? How can you rank the likelihood of different events on a scale from never to always?

In this lesson, students apply what they are learning about chance to real-world events. Students use probability lines and qualitative descriptions (such as *never, likely,* and *always*) to describe and rank the likelihood of different events' happening on a typical school day. They then explore ways of representing the probabilities of the events in numbers (such as ½, .33, and 75%). Students apply these numerical expressions when they calculate the probabilities for events in a class raffle and place the events on a probability line. In a final activity, students investigate an example of how probabilities are used in real-world situations by examining an advertisement based on weather statistics.

Mathematical Goals

- Describe probabilities using qualitative terms.
- Describe probabilities quantitatively using decimals, fractions, percents, and ratios.
- Rank the probability of events on a scale of 0 to 1.
- Use a probability line to represent and compare the likelihoods of events.

Materials

Per Pair

Reproducible 8, *How Likely Is It?*

Reproducible 9, *Hoping for Snow*

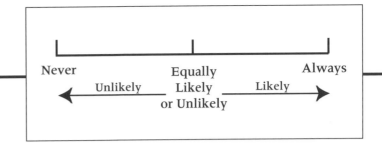

Never	Equally	Always
Unlikely	Likely	Likely
	or Unlikely	

Suggested Lesson Plan

1. Problem Solving: *How would you rank the likelihood of different real-world events?*

Reproducible 8

Students work in pairs on *How Likely Is It?* (Reproducible 8). They discuss events that might happen during a day at school and rank the events from never to always by placing them on a probability line.

Have students compare their probability lines in groups or in a class discussion. Through the comparisons, students think further about the relationship between probability and real-world events. They also see how different people will rank events differently, depending on their own experiences. Some questions to guide the discussion include:

- What events did you add to the probability line? Where did you place them?
- How did you decide where to place each event on your probability line?
- Give some examples of events for each of the following: (a) definitely happen; (b) probably happen; (c) probably not happen; and (d) never happen.

▶ **From the Classroom**

I decided to start the lesson with a whole-class brainstorming session. I drew an unlabeled probability line on the board and asked students to brainstorm things that would "always" happen or things that would "never" happen. The students enjoyed suggesting events for placement on the line, and it prepared them for the activities in the lesson.

▶ *When we discussed events that would never happen, many students would phrase the event in the negative, as in "dogs won't fly." The double negative of "dogs won't fly" will "never" happen, confused a few students, particularly those who were not native speakers of English. I found it helpful to restate these suggestions as questions for the class: "Do you agree that dogs' flying is something that will never happen?" I then asked them where to place it on the probability line.*

Some students thought that if an event might or might not happen, then it had a 50% probability and belonged in the middle of the probability line. For example, "Our locker won't open." "It will rain tomorrow." "Mr. G. will tell a bad joke." I pointed out that, in these cases, the chances of the event's happening were not necessarily the same as the chances of its not happening. In fact, few events have a 50-50 chance of happening.

► *Students came up with 0 to represent things that would "Never" happen, but they were not as certain about the numerical representation for things that "Definitely" happen, suggesting "100," "1000," and "Infinity" as possible representations. One student suggested that −1 was the oppposite of 0. I pointed out that 1 is a numerical representation of things that will definitely happen and reminded them that 100% = 1. From there students were able to see that ¹/₂ or .5 would be the numerical representation of "Equally Likely or Unlikely" on the probability line.*

2. Discussion: *How can you use percents, fractions, and decimals to describe some of the events on your probability line?*

Using the probability lines they made in Step 1, students consider ways of using numbers to describe events:

- Which events on your probability line do you think would happen 100% of the time? why?
- About what percent of the time do you think the other events would happen?
- How could you use fractions and decimals to describe the probabilities of events?

Introduce the following points if students do not raise them in the discussion:

- The probability that a specific event will occur is the ratio of the number of times that event occurs to the number of total possible occurrences.
- Events that are impossible and will never happen have a probability of zero, or 0% and events that are definite and will always happen have a probability of one, or 100%.
- A probability can never be greater than one, or 100%, because it's impossible to have a ratio with more of a specific event than the total possible events.

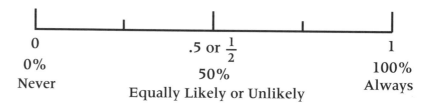

0		.5 or $\frac{1}{2}$		1
0%		50%		100%
Never		Equally Likely or Unlikely		Always

3. Problem Solving: *Make a probability line for a class raffle.*

Students determine the probabilities of different events at a class raffle. This activity works well for homework.

4. Problem Solving: *What are the chances it will snow on New Year's Eve?*

Students examine an actual jewelry store advertisement from a Massachusetts newspaper, which is reprinted on *Hoping for Snow* (Reproducible 9). Students discuss ways of figuring out the probability of getting a refund. Then, they design their own advertisements that involve probability. Similar advertisements were run by stores across the country. You may want to substitute one of the advertisements below if it is more appropriate for your area.

A. Let It Rain! You'll receive a 100% REFUND for jewelry purchases if it rains 2 or more inches on December 31.

B. The Hotter the Better! You'll receive a 100% REFUND for jewelry purchases if December 31st is the hottest day of the month.

In our school, the eighth-grade students were holding a fund-raising raffle. Most of the students in the class had purchased tickets, and I asked them what were the chances of winning. We knew that each of the 67 eighth-grade students had been responsible for selling 15 tickets and that they were raffling off 50 prizes. Maria suggested that we calculate the total number of tickets sold, which they did and decided to round-off to 1,000. Paul suggested that we divide the number of tickets sold by the number of prizes, and soon announced to the class that "there's one prize for every twenty tickets." Monica focused on how people's chances differed depending on the number of tickets they had purchased: "I bought 5 tickets, each with a 1/20 chance. That's 5 over 20 or a 1 in 4 chance of winning. I've got a 25% chance of winning."

Reproducible 9

Note: The jewelry store that ran the advertisement was insured by a weather insurance agency called Worldwide Weather. If it snowed 3 or more inches on New Year's Eve (1993), the insurance company would give the store the money to make refunds to all the customers. To get the insurance, the store owner paid a percentage of her profits for November and December to the insurance company. As it turned out, it didn't snow in Massachusetts on December 31, 1993. However, Worldwide Weather did provide refund money to customers in the Carribean when an advertisement like B above was run and December 31st was the hottest day of the month.

Worldwide Weather uses computer data bases with historical weather information from 50,000 locations worldwide to determine the probabilities of different weather conditions, such as amount of rainfall, consecutive dry hours, amount of snow fall, wind speed, and maximum, minimum, or average temperatures. The company also provides weather insurance for outdoor filming, outdoor concerts, sports events, vacations, fairs, and parades. For example, the organizers of an outdoor rock concert have figured out that if it rains they will need to give out $10,000 in ticket refunds. The insurance company determines the probability of rain for the date and location and uses that information to set the cost of insurance.

5. Problem Solving: *Make a probability line for an activity you know well.*

Students create probability lines for familiar situations. This activity works well for homework.

TO THE STUDENT

- Pick an activity or situation you know well. For example, you could choose getting ready for school in the morning, playing a sport, or going shopping.
- Make a list of at least 6 events that might happen in the activity. Try to think of events that have different chances of happening.
- Order the events by putting them on a probability line.

Never	Equally Likely or Unlikely	Always

- How did you determine where to put the events on the probability line?

My students really enjoyed this activity. I assigned it for homework and was very pleased when everyone did it—even my students who never do their homework. They made probability lines for a wide range of topics of interest to them, including dancing, shopping at the mall, playing the piano, walking a dog, and playing basketball. I was thrilled with the level of creativity and effort they demonstrated. I also learned a bit about their interests and personalities from looking at their probability lines. As a math teacher, I very rarely get to learn about my students. It's interesting to get to know them!

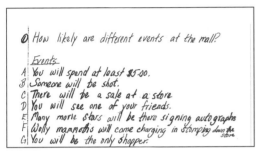

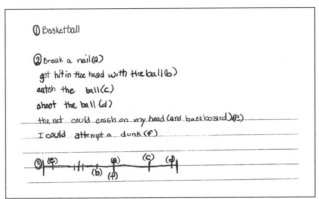

Homework Possibilities

Problem Solving

Hoping for Snow (Reproducible 9) works well as homework.

Writing

Dr. Math letter E (Appendix A).

Drawing

Students draw pictures to communicate the meaning of the word chance.

Data Collection

Students make a list of terms and expressions that are used for describing the likelihood of events, such as *fat chance, once in a blue moon, in your dreams, when there's snow in August,* and *sure thing.* Students can develop their list by brainstorming with classmates, by interviewing people in their community, and/or looking for examples in newspapers and magazines. Students may want to include words from different languages.

Spinner Games: Multiple Representations of Probability

The section focuses on circular spinners, which serve both as game pieces and as visual models of probability. Unlike the coins and cubes students explored in Section 1, spinners can be designed to produce—and represent—events with unequal probabilities. In the Cover-Up game introduced in Lesson 4, students experiment with spinners with unequal probabilities and test their predictions. In Lesson 5, they move on to playing Mystery Spinner games in which they create spinners that match clues describing probabilities in numbers and words. In Lesson 6, students create their own clues for Mystery Spinner games. At the end of Lesson 6, students are assessed on their ability to interpret and express numeric, verbal, and visual representations of probabilities.

The Game Piece Lab in the optional *Chance Encounters* software enables students to create simulated objects in which the outcomes have unequal probabilities (such as a coin that will land on heads 75% of the time) and conduct experiments with these objects. The Cover-Up Game Lab and related activities then allow students to collect data quickly from many replays of a game. Students can use this lab to explore ways to optimize their game cards and to explore using spinners with various configurations of probabilities.

Approx. # of Classes	Lessons
1–2	**4. The Cover-Up Game** Students explore the probabilities in a game played with a circular spinner divided into unequal parts. They experiment with ways of changing the game to improve their chances of winning.
2	**5. Mystery Spinners** Students work in groups to design spinners to match a set of clues describing probabilities in words and numbers.
2	**6. Designing Mystery Spinner Games** Students design their own mystery spinner games. They exchange games with their classmates.

Lesson summary and sample schedule for Section 2

Mathematical Themes

- Determine the theoretical probability of events.
- Distinguish events that have equal probabilities from events that have unequal probabilities.
- Conduct probability experiments, including collecting, representing, and analyzing data.

Theoretical and Experimental Probability

The section focuses on circular spinners, which provide a clear visual model of theoretical probability: The relative size of each section of the spinner is the theoretical probability of that section. For example, on the spinner below, green occupies half the spinner and so it has a probability of .5. Yellow and pink each occupy one-fourth the spinner, so they each have a probability of .25.

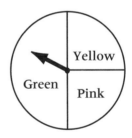

When students play the Cover-Up game in Lesson 4, they are given a spinner with unequal probabilities and asked to create a game card. To play the game well, the number of each item put on the card should reflect the theoretical probability of its occurrence. Students collect experimental data to compare the number of spins needed to cover their game cards, and relate the theoretical and experimental probabilities.

Through the Mystery Spinner activities in Lessons 5 and 6, students expand their understanding of theoretical probabilities by learning to express them in verbal, visual, and numeric representations.

Multiple Representations of Probability

- Explore area models of probability.
- Describe probabilities as fractions, percents, decimals, and ratios.
- Describe probabilities with qualitative terms, such as *least likely* and *most likely.*
- Relate verbal, visual, and numeric representations of probability.
- Gain an understanding of the meaning of a probability of 1, or 100%.

In providing a clear visual model of probability, circular spinners help students explore the relationships among various representations of probability. In playing the Mystery Spinner games, for example, students relate verbal and numeric representations of probability to the area model provided by the spinners. When they design their own games, students describe probabilities with qualitative and quantitative terms so that another student would have enough information to draw the spinner accurately.

Working with the Cover-Up and Mystery Spinner games also helps students recognize that the sum of all the probabilities of the spinner parts would make a complete spinner, which represented numerically is 100%, or 1.

Modeling Situations with Simulations

Students continue to add to the repertoire of concepts and techniques they will need to analyze and create simulations in Section 4. In particular, spinners enable students to simulate events that have unequal probabilities, and the various representations provide ways for students to describe the data upon which their simulations will be based.

*Giving and
Receiving Feedback*

After students had designed their own mystery spinner games, I divided the class into pairs to test each other's games. I assigned pairs somewhat randomly, but tried to think about who would work well together. I didn't want students to pick their own partners because I thought that if they worked with their friends, they wouldn't be objective and would be more inclined to say that the games worked well even if they didn't. I instructed students to swap games with their partners, try to solve the games, and then complete the Test a Mystery Spinner Game sheets.

As soon as students exchanged games and started working, I realized that this activity was going to be more difficult for them than I had anticipated. Several students had trouble critiquing someone else's work. They didn't see themselves as game testers with the job of giving feedback to help the designers revise the games. Instead, they thought the challenge was to solve the games. This was certainly understandable since they had spent the previous two days successfully solving most of the mystery spinner games. To them, this was simply another mystery spinner game to solve. Students were upset when they couldn't solve the games, either because there were essential clues missing or because they were simply too hard.

I had asked students to work independently and not to discuss the games with their partners until they had finished testing the games, but most of my students couldn't hold back their questions and comments: "What do you mean by this clue?" "This doesn't make sense." Some students were able to offer constructive feedback. Johanna, for example, quietly tested her partner's game and offered thoughtful, useful suggestions. She made a note that his game used phrases that were difficult to understand. For example, in one clue he referred to the "lower part" of the spinner, and she wasn't sure if he was referring to the bottom half of the circle or the smaller part.

Other students were more confrontational, especially the pairs who don't seem to get along with each other very well. Corey, for example, couldn't solve Jack's game, although there was really nothing wrong with the clues. He insisted that the game couldn't be solved, but couldn't identify the problem. When Jack eventually showed him how to solve the game, he thought he was successful because he had "stumped" the tester. Jack announced proudly, "Ha! Gotcha! He couldn't solve mine!"

Melissa and James were arguing about James's game. Melissa couldn't figure out his game and asked him to clarify one of the clues. After the two argued for a few minutes, she said, "Forget him!" and stormed away. Frustrated, he asked, "What could be more clear than what I wrote?"

I spent most of the period putting out fires. I walked around the room reminding students that their role was to help each other improve the games, not to make each other feel bad.

Looking back on what happened, I realized that in presenting the lesson to students, I had emphasized their solving a mystery spinner game by themselves more than I had stressed and supported their learning to give and receive feedback. After solving so many games in groups, I wanted my students to solve a game independently. I also wanted them to "correct" their games. Now I realize it would have been better to have students focus on analyzing games and on providing constructive feedback. I could have just as easily saved one of the mystery spinner games from the previous lesson for them to solve independently.

Although my students had some problems with this lesson, it raised a lot of interesting social dynamics, and helped me understand my class better. It alerted me that they are not used to giving each other feedback in math class. Since I think learning to give and receive feedback is important, I didn't want to give up. I also didn't want another session like this one. I realized that if I wanted to make this process work in my classroom, I would have to help them create a more friendly, helpful environment. I decided that in the future I would let my students pick their own partners, and take a more "buddy, buddy" approach to working together and giving and receiving feedback. With another class, I might take a different approach, but this seems like the best strategy for these students.

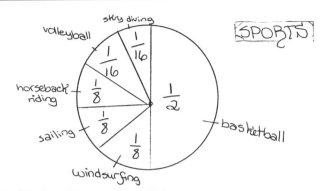

1. How difficult was the game to solve? Circle your answer.

   Very Easy   Easy   Medium   Difficult   (Very Difficult)   Impossible

2. What made the game easy or difficult to solve?
   The game needed a lot of figuring out. It just gave us 2 parts and based on the confusing directions we had to figure 4 things out. It involved a lot of thinking & great concentration.

3. Were you missing any information? If so, what information would you want to get from the clues? We were missing the information of sailing, sky diving horseback riding & volleyball. We had to get & figure out the parts for each clue.

4. What did you like about the game? What suggestions would you like to give to the designers? I thought the game was complicated which made it fun. I would suggest that in order to make it harder that they would need 10 types of sports. I liked their clues.

A student's feedback on a classmate's game.

Lesson 4

The Cover-Up Game

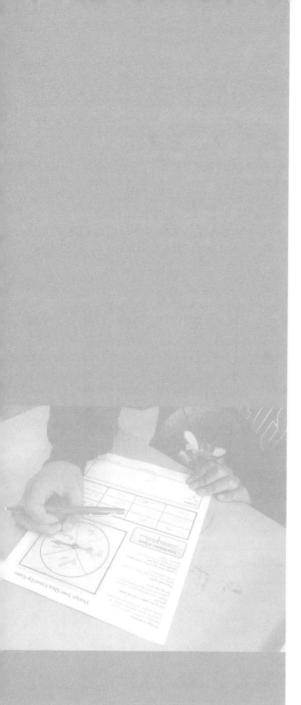

How can you determine the chances that the arrow of a spinner will stop on a particular part of the circle?

Students begin investigating games played with circular spinners that have unequal parts. In the Cover-Up game, students spin a spinner and then "cover up" the corresponding box on a game card divided into equal parts, four boxes for each of the three colors on the spinner. How many spins will it take to cover the game card?

The contrast between the game card and the spinner brings out the differences between events with equal likelihood and those with unequal likelihood. After analyzing results for the Cover-Up game, students design new game cards that will improve their chances of finishing the game in the fewest spins. As they decide how many of the 12 boxes on the game card to give to each color, students explore the probabilities for each part of the spinner. Students test their new game cards and share their results with their classmates. They then design their own version of the game, including a new spinner and a new game card.

Students will continue their investigation of spinners in Lessons 5 and 6, when they create spinners to match qualitative and quantitive descriptions of specific probabilities.

Mathematical Goals

- Determine the theoretical probability of events.
- Distinguish events that have equal probabilities from events that have unequal probabilities.
- Conduct probability experiments.
- Explore area models of probability.

Spinner

Red
Blue
Blue
Yellow

Game Card

B	B	B	B
R	R	R	R
Y	Y	Y	Y

Materials

Per Pair

Reproducible 10,
Cover-Up Game

Reproducible 11,
Spinner Possibilities

Reproducible 12,
Design Your Own Game

Spinner (see preparation
section below)

Per Class

Reproducible 10, *Cover-Up
Game* (optional transparency)

Several rolls of removable
tape or masking tape for
attaching transparent
spinners to templates

Preparation

Transparent spinners, which can be ordered from most educational supply catalogs, can be taped to different spinner templates. These spinners also tend to be more reliable and sturdier than handmade ones. As a lower-cost alternative, it is possible to make a spinner by using a paper clip and a pencil or ball-point pen.

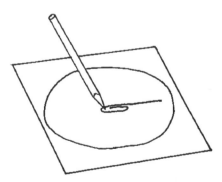

One student holds the pencil while
the other spins the paper clip.

Suggested Lesson Plan

1. Investigation: *How many spins will it take to finish the Cover-Up Game?*

Cover-Up Game (Reproducible 10) provides the rules, spinner, and scoresheet for the game. You may want to display the reproducible on an overhead and demonstrate how to play a few turns and "cover up" the game card. Cover-Up is similar to Bingo and Lotto.

How to Play the Cover-Up Game

Each time the spinner lands on a color, players get to check or cross off a matching color on their game card.

For example, if the spinner lands on yellow, you can cross off one of the yellow boxes on your card.

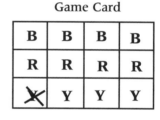

Spinner

Game Card

B	B	B	B
R	R	R	R
X̶	Y	Y	Y

Goal: To cross off all the boxes in the *fewest* number of spins. You do *not* need to cross off the boxes in order.

Extras: Keep track of the number of Extra colors that you spin. An Extra is a color that you do *not* need.

For example, if all the yellow boxes are crossed off and you spin a yellow, then the yellow is scored as an extra.

Game Card

B	B	B	B
R	R	R	R
X̶	X̶	X̶	X̶

Extras

Blue	Red	Yellow
		/

In testing the Cover-Up game, students work in pairs to investigate how many spins or trials it takes to reach a specific outcome: the number of reds, blues, and yellows on their game card. Unlike the game-testing activities in Section 1, the question is not How many of each color will you get in 20 spins? but rather, How many spins will it take to get four of each color? Students will use what they learn about the game to improve the game card and, later, design their own version of the game.

Having students play the game without first discussing the spinner allows students to construct their own understanding of the relationship between the spinner parts and the game card. To shorten the investigation, set a maximum number of spins. For example, with a maximum of 30 spins, the game ends when students have covered their cards *or* had 30 spins.

2. Discussion: *How do your results compare with those of your classmates? What is the range of spins in the class?*

Compile the class data so that students can compare the number of spins it took to finish the game.

How many spins did it take to cover our cards?

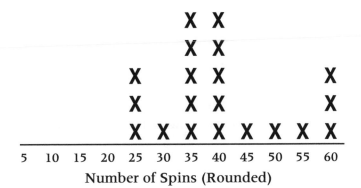

Number of Spins (Rounded)

X = one pair of students

Some questions for analyzing the results include:

- What is the range of number of spins in the class? How are they distributed? Are they clumped together or spread out?
- How do your game results compare with your classmates' results?
- Which color extras did you get the most of? How does that compare with your classmates?
- If you played again with the same spinner, how would you fill in a game card with 24 boxes? 48? 100? why?

▶ From the Classroom

My students were surprised by the wide range of results in the class. One student covered his card in only 15 spins while another took a frustrating 52 spins to finish. Students agreed that the game would be more fun to play if it usually took less than 25 spins to finish.

A few students got more yellows than blues, which was not what they had expected. They thought that the largest part would come up the most in every game. I suggested students investigate this further by doing an experiment in which they each did 50 spins.

3. Investigation: *Design a new game card to improve chances of finishing the game in fewer spins.*

Students apply what they have learned to creating new game cards.

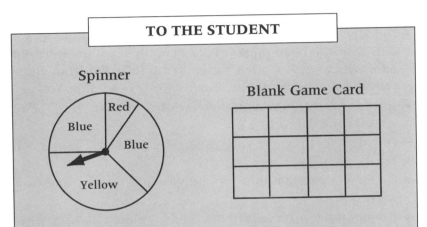

TO THE STUDENT

Spinner

Blank Game Card

Based on your results, the game designers at the AllPlay Company want to change the game card for The Cover-Up game. They think the game would be more fun if it didn't take so many spins to finish. They don't want to change the spinners, though; the factory has already made 10,000 of them.

1. Design a game card that gives players a good chance of finishing the Cover-Up Game in the fewest spins.

   Make a game card with 12 boxes. How many boxes of each color do you want in your game card? Write the name of a color (red, yellow, or blue) in each of the 12 boxes. You do not need to use all the colors.

2. Make predictions.

   Before you play, predict how many spins it will take you to cover your card.

3. Play the game and record your results (including keeping track of the extras).

   How do your results compare with your predictions?

There are multiple ways to fill in the game cards. In general, the cards should show more blues and yellows than reds. A card with 7 blue boxes, 4 yellow, and 1 red would be in proportion to the areas of the spinner parts. Some students may want to leave red off the game cards altogether because the chances of spinning red are small.

4. Discussion: *What happened when you tested your new game cards?*

Display students' game cards so that they can be compared. During the discussion, you may want to try sorting and arranging the cards in different ways to emphasize different kinds of comparisons. For example, you may group the cards by the number of spins or the number of reds.

- Did any students finish in the same number of spins as you did? How do the numbers of colors on their game cards compare with yours? If their game card is different from yours, why did they finish in the same number of spins as you did?
- How do your results with the new card compare with the results for the old card?
- Did anyone do worse with the new game card? Why might that happen?
- If you played again, how would you fill in your game card? why?
- Do you think a game card that had 12 blues would give you a good chance of finishing in the fewest spins? why or why not?
- Is it possible to make a game card for your spinner that you could cover in 12 spins every time you played?

▶ **From the Classroom**

I had students use colored pens to make larger versions of their game cards and to write the total number of spins in the corner of the card. Students posted their cards on the chalkboard and then I asked the class how they wanted to sort the cards—according to the number of total spins or according to how similar the cards looked. They voted to sort them according to the number of spins, which ranged from 12 to 23. The sorted cards helped get the discussion off to a fast start. Students could easily see that the most popular number of spins was 15, and that these cards had "a lot of blues and yellows," and few or no reds. They also saw that the cards with the higher numbers of spins tended to have more reds. One student explained that the cards with "about half blues and about ⅜ yellow" got the lowest number of spins.

▶ *A few of my students reported that they got 12 and 13 total spins, which prompted other students to accuse them of cheating. Although I was pleased that they realized that getting 12 spins would be very unlikely, I was not sure how to handle the ongoing accusations. I reminded the class that the purpose of the activity is to investigate the game, not to win.*

It is not possible to make a game card
that you could cover up in 12 turns every time
you played, because the game is always about
chance. Everytime you play you have a chance
of covering up the board in 12 turns, but most
of the time it doesn't happen because that
chance is very little. If two people played the

same board and one person covers up the
board in 12 turns doesn't mean the other will

Good Response

A) spin lightly or really hard depending
on which color you want B) Never write
a lot of the same color when filling
out a grid

Misconception

5. Problem Solving: *How can you draw spinners to reflect specific probabilities?*

On *Spinner Possibilities* (Reproducible 11), students explore different ways of describing the chances of spinning each of the colors using numbers and words, such as "Red, yellow, and blue have the same chances of being spun." When they create spinners to match various descriptions, students explore the relationship between the size of spinner parts and probabilities.

This is a good homework option.

6. Investigation: *Design your own cover-up game.*

Using *Design Your Own Cover-Up Game* (Reproducible 12), students create both a spinner and a game card that will give them a good chance of finishing the game in the fewest spins.

A variation on the activity that may help highlight the relationship between the spinner and the game card is to have students design two different game cards to go with the spinner. One of the cards should give players a *good* chance of finishing the game in the fewest spins. The other card should give players a *poor* chance of finishing in the fewest spins, but it should still be possible to cross off the game card.

This activity, which can be done in pairs or individually, is a good homework option.

Reproducible 11

Reproducible 12

► **From the Classroom**

Since I'm always looking ahead to the next lessons, I really liked this activity. It gave students an initial experience with spinners and led them nicely into designing their own spinners.

ASSESSMENT CRITERIA

Do students' games show that they understand:

- *That the parts of circular spinners with larger areas tend to be spun more often than parts with smaller areas?*
- *That parts of a circular spinner that have the same area are equally likely to be spun?*

► **From the Classroom**

My students liked being able to create their own games, but some of them had so many parts on their spinners that they couldn't make a game card that accurately reflected the probabilities. I decided to limit the spinners to either three or four parts.

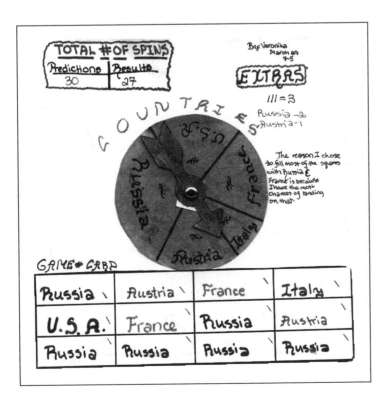

Homework Possibilities

Problem Solving

Both *Spinner Possibilities* (Reproducible 11) and *Design Your Own Cover-Up Game* (Reproducible 12) work well as homework.

Writing

Dr. Math letters F–H (Appendix A).

Software Possibilities

The *Chance Encounters* software provides many opportunities for students to extend their investigation of the Cover-Up Game. They can simulate running a series of experiments with 12 spins to explore the variability of results with a small number of trials. They can also conduct multiple trials with different numbers of spins to see which numbers would enable them to cover their cards 50% of the time. Additionally, they can investigate how changing the size of the spinner parts, the ways of filling in the game card, and the number of spins affect the results.

Background Information on the Cover-Up Game

The probability of getting each spinner part is red, $\frac{1}{12}$; blue, $\frac{7}{12}$; and yellow, $\frac{4}{12}$. However, filling the game card with 1 red box, 7 blues, and 4 yellows does not guarantee finishing the game in 12 spins. Given the small number of trials in the game, the variability of results will be large. The table below shows the results of 20 experiments in which the spinner was spun 12 times. The results of 1 red, 7 blues, and 4 yellows came up in only two of the experiments (as indicated by asterisks below).

Experiment # (Each Has 12 Spins)	Number of Reds Spun	Number of Blues Spun	Number of Yellows Spun
1.	1	10	1
2.	2	4	6
3.	2	7	3
4.	1	10	1
5.	3	7	2
6.	0	5	7
7.	0	7	5
8.	2	7	3
9.	0	7	5
10.	1	6	5
11.*	1	7	4
12.	1	8	3
13.	2	5	5
14.	2	5	5
15.	1	6	5
16.	1	6	5
17.	2	6	4
18.*	1	7	4
19.	2	7	3
20.	2	6	4
Average Times Each Color was Spun	1.35	6.65	4
Range of Times Spun	0–3	4–10	1–7

Lesson 5

Mystery Spinners

How can you design a spinner to match probabilities described in words and numbers?

In the Mystery Spinner games, students work in groups to create a circular spinner from a set of clues. The clues describe the probabilities of each spinner section in words and numbers, such as *You are more likely to spin red than yellow* or *You will probably get yellow 25% of the time.* As students solve the clues and draw a whole spinner, they explore the relationships among verbal, numerical, and visual representations of probability. The lesson ends with an assessment of students' understanding of Mystery Spinner games.

In Lesson 6, students will design their own spinners and clues.

Mathematical Goals

Solve problems by:

- Representing probabilities as areas.
- Understanding probabilities expressed as fractions, percents, decimals, and ratios.
- Relating verbal, visual, and numeric representations of probability.
- Using logical reasoning.

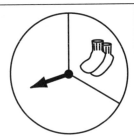

You are likely to win socks about 10 times in 30 spins.

Materials

Per Student

Reproducible 16, *Spinner Solitaire*

Per Group

Reproducible 14, *Mystery Spinner Games* (4 sheets)

Envelopes or small bags (for storing sets of clues)

Reproducible 15, *Spinner Design Kit* (optional)

Scissors for use with *Spinner Design Kit* (optional)

Per Class

Reproducible 13, *Mystery Spinner Game Rules* (transparency)

Preparation

There are nine Mystery Spinner games, each with a set of four clues. Make enough copies of the clues so that each group of four students will have the opportunity to play three or more of the games. One possibility is to make enough copies for half the groups in the class. When a group finishes game 1, they switch clues with a group that has finished game 2, and so on.

Cut out the clues and separate them into sets, using envelopes or small bags. You may want to laminate the clues to preserve them for use in future years.

If your students do not have a lot of experience working with fractions, you may want to make two copies of *Spinner Design Kit* (Reproducible 15) for each group.

Suggested Lesson Plan

1. Introduction: *How is the Mystery Spinner Game played?*

Using *Mystery Spinner Game Rules* (Reproducible 13), introduce the game and have the whole class solve the sample set of clues. Explain that group members read the clues aloud but do not show their clues to one another. This rule prevents one group member from taking over all the clues and solving the game alone. By labeling the spinner parts with fractions or percents, students make the connection between numerical and visual representations of probabilities. The label also helps clarify the size of the spinner parts, since the spinners are drawn freehand (without protractors).

▶ **From the Classroom**

I revealed the clues for the sample game one by one on the overhead and asked students to draw spinners to match the clues. When the class decided on a solution, we went back through the list to check that it fit the clues.

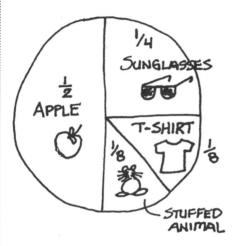

It took about two games for the groups to figure out how to work together. Some of the groups selected a recorder to draw the spinner as the group solved the clues. Others decided to solve the clues as a group, but had each student draw the spinner. This latter method seemed to work much better. Since each student was drawing a spinner, they were less likely to let one student do all the work. These groups also avoided arguments about how neatly the recorder was drawing the spinner.

#13, Lesson 5

Mystery Spinner Game Rules

Number of Players: 4

Rules:

- Each player gets one clue.

- Players read the clues aloud to the group. They **cannot** show their clues to one another.

- The group needs to draw *one* spinner that matches all the players' clues.

- Label the parts of the spinner with fractions or percents.

- Check to make sure the spinner matches all the clues.

Sample Game
Clues:

A. The spinner has the 4 kinds of prizes. You are likely to win an apple about 50% of the time.

B. You will probably get sunglasses about $\frac{1}{4}$ of the time.

C. In 80 spins, you will probably get a T-shirt about 10 times.

D. You have the same chances of getting a stuffed animal as getting a T-shirt.

Reproducible 13   *Chance Encounters*   ©EDC, 1995

Reproducible 13

2. Problem Solving: *Play the Mystery Spinner Game.*

The nine Mystery Spinner games are numbered in increasing order of difficulty. Each group of students should play at least three of the games. To ensure that everyone understands the games, have all students play games 1 and/or 2 before moving on to the other games.

If your students do not have a lot of experience working with fractions, you may want to have students use the *Spinner Design Kit* (Reproducible 15) when they play the game. The kit provides blank spinners marked with 12ths, 16ths, 20ths, and 24ths so that students do not have to create freehand spinners. Students cut the blank spinners into parts and then assemble the parts to create a spinner that matches the clues. This variation of the game gives students a sense of the relative sizes of fractions and provides a way for students to check whether the parts make a whole (a complete spinner) without having to do any calculations. After playing several games with the manipulatives, students can move on to drawing the spinners.

The solutions to the games are shown at the end of the lesson.

3. Writing: *What strategies did you use to draw the mystery spinners?*

Encourage students to reflect on the thinking their group used to interpret the clues and design spinners. You may also want to have students write about how well the group worked together.

- What kinds of clues make good starting points?
- What strategies did you use to come up with one spinner that matched all the clues?
- How can you prove that your spinner matches all the clues?

Reproducibles 14 & 15

► **From the Classroom**

Some students tried to draw the spinner before they heard all the clues, which led to a lot of false starts and erasing. One group was trying to solve game 8 based on only the first two clues:

> *Brian (reading clue): The chances of getting a bicycle are half the chances of getting a bus.*
> *Alisha: So, it has to be $\frac{1}{6}$.*
> *Carlos: Mine says, "You have a 1 in 12 probability of getting an airplane."*
> *Alisha: No. It has to be $\frac{1}{6}$.*
> *Carlos: Oh, there are more than 4 vehicles!*
> *Dina: Well, if you would listen to mine, it says there are 5 vehicles!*

► *My students realized that they didn't know as much about fractions as they thought. Many were unsure how to draw thirds and sixths. If they made these parts too large, they ran into difficulties because there wasn't enough room for the other spinner parts. Other students incorrectly assumed that if a spinner part was small it had to be a sixteenth. To address these misconceptions, I decided to have students play a few games by cutting out parts from the Spinner Design Kit.*

► **From the Classroom**

While we were discussing the kinds of clues that make good starting points, one student explained that her group began by reading the clues and deciding what the smallest fraction was. They then divided the spinner into that many parts.

► *One group realized they had space left over on a spinner they thought they had completed. This provided a nice lead-in to a discussion of how students could make sure that their spinners matched all of the clues. Students explained that one way to check is to add all of the parts of the spinner together. The sum had to equal 1 if the parts were labeled in fractions, or 100% if they were using percents.*

4. Assessment: *Solve Mystery Spinner games individually.*

Students work individually to solve the clue sets on *Spinner Solitaire* (Reproducible 16). This assessment will help you target areas in which students are having problems before you do the more formal assessment in Lesson 6. The games are numbered in increasing order of difficulty.

This activity is a good homework option. Answers are provided at the end of the lesson.

Homework Possibilities

Problem Solving

- *Spinner Solitaire* (Reproducible 16) works well as homework.
- You may want students to solve some of the higher-numbered Mystery Spinner games (such as games 6–9) individually for homework.

Practice

This activity provides students with more practice determining whether the parts of a spinner make a whole. It also helps address the misconception that if a spinner is divided into 4 parts, then each part must be $\frac{1}{4}$.

TO THE STUDENT

1. Find different ways to make spinners that have 4 parts.
   a. Cut out parts from your Spinner Design Kit and put them together to make spinners. Try to make at least 8 different spinners that have 4 parts.
   b. Record all the ways you find. Label the parts of each spinner with fractions or percents.
2. Can the parts listed below be used to make complete spinners? If possible, draw a spinner for each set and label the parts. If the parts do not make a complete spinner, explain why. Add or replace a part to fix the spinner.
   a. $\frac{1}{2}$ $\frac{1}{4}$ $\frac{1}{8}$ $\frac{1}{8}$ b. $\frac{1}{3}$ $\frac{1}{4}$ $\frac{1}{6}$ c. $\frac{3}{8}$ $\frac{1}{4}$ $\frac{1}{6}$ $\frac{5}{16}$
   d. $\frac{1}{2}$ $\frac{1}{3}$ $\frac{1}{6}$ e. $\frac{1}{3}$ $\frac{1}{12}$ $\frac{3}{4}$

Answers

Mystery Spinner Games

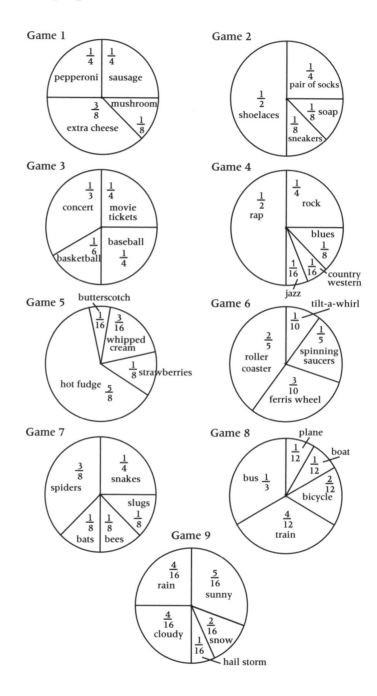

Game 1

$\frac{1}{4}$ pepperoni $\frac{1}{4}$ sausage $\frac{3}{8}$ extra cheese mushroom $\frac{1}{8}$

Game 2

$\frac{1}{4}$ pair of socks $\frac{1}{2}$ shoelaces $\frac{1}{8}$ soap $\frac{1}{8}$ sneakers

Game 3

$\frac{1}{3}$ concert $\frac{1}{4}$ movie tickets $\frac{1}{6}$ basketball baseball $\frac{1}{4}$

Game 4

$\frac{1}{2}$ rap $\frac{1}{4}$ rock blues $\frac{1}{8}$ $\frac{1}{16}$ $\frac{1}{16}$ country western jazz

Game 5

butterscotch $\frac{1}{16}$ $\frac{3}{16}$ whipped cream $\frac{1}{8}$ strawberries hot fudge $\frac{5}{8}$

Game 6

tilt-a-whirl $\frac{1}{10}$ $\frac{1}{5}$ $\frac{2}{5}$ roller coaster spinning saucers $\frac{3}{10}$ ferris wheel

Game 7

$\frac{3}{8}$ spiders $\frac{1}{4}$ snakes slugs $\frac{1}{8}$ bats $\frac{1}{8}$ bees $\frac{1}{8}$

Game 8

plane $\frac{1}{12}$ boat $\frac{1}{12}$ bus $\frac{1}{3}$ $\frac{2}{12}$ bicycle $\frac{4}{12}$ train

Game 9

$\frac{4}{16}$ rain $\frac{5}{16}$ sunny $\frac{4}{16}$ cloudy $\frac{2}{16}$ snow $\frac{1}{16}$ hail storm

Spinner Solitaire

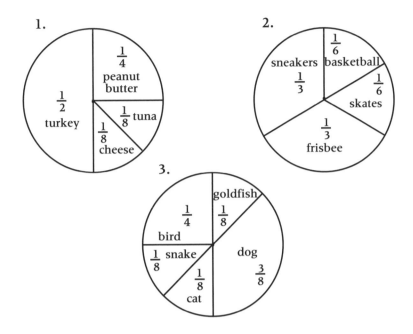

1.
- $\frac{1}{4}$ peanut butter
- $\frac{1}{2}$ turkey
- $\frac{1}{8}$ tuna
- $\frac{1}{8}$ cheese

2.
- $\frac{1}{6}$ basketball
- sneakers $\frac{1}{3}$
- $\frac{1}{6}$ skates
- $\frac{1}{3}$ frisbee

3.
- goldfish $\frac{1}{8}$
- $\frac{1}{4}$ bird
- $\frac{1}{8}$ snake
- $\frac{1}{8}$ cat
- dog $\frac{3}{8}$

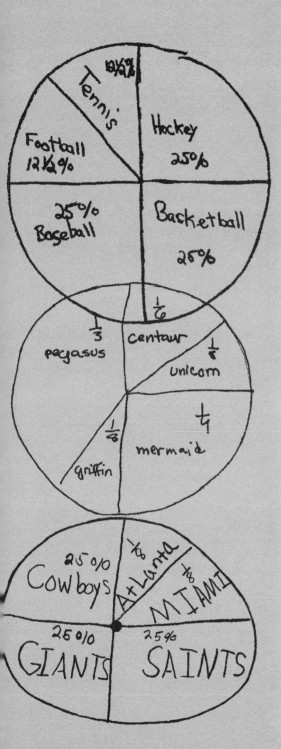

Designing Mystery Spinner Games

Can you write a set of clues that another student could use to create a spinner?

This lesson serves as an assessment of what students have learned in this section about qualitative and quantitative descriptions of probability. Students begin by examining and fixing two flawed Mystery Spinner games, which helps prepare them for designing their own game. To design a game, students write a set of clues that (1) describe probabilities in a variety of ways and (2) provide all the information another student would need to draw a complete spinner. Students play each other's games and provide feedback on how the games might be improved. They then use the suggestions to revise the games. The lesson ends with an assessment in which students complete a series of unfinished spinner games.

Mathematical Goals

Apply and extend knowledge of:
- Representing probabilities as areas.
- Describing probabilities as fractions, percents, decimals, and ratios.
- Relating verbal, visual, and numeric representations of probability.

Materials

Per Student	Per Pair	Per Class
Reproducible 19, *Unfinished Games*	Reproducible 18, *Design Your Own Mystery Spinner Game*	Reproducible 17, *What's Wrong with These Games?* (transparency)
		Reproducible 18, *Design Your Own Mystery Spinner Game* (transparency)

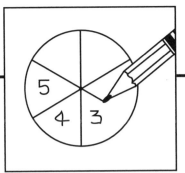

Suggested Lesson Plan

1. Problem Solving: *How would you fix these mystery spinner games?*

The process of evaluating and fixing the flawed clues on Reproducible 17 helps students articulate what they have learned about spinners and probabilities. It also helps prepare them for designing their own games. This activity can be done individually or in small groups.

Solutions are provided at the end of the lesson.

#17, Lesson 6

What's Wrong with These Games?

Figure out what's wrong with the games below. Change the clues to fix the problems.

Game 1

A. You have the highest chance of winning a bike.

B. The chances of winning a skateboard are $\frac{1}{16}$.

C. Car has the same chances as skateboard.

D. Motorcycle has the same chances as roller blades.

E. You have a 50% chance of winning roller blades.

Game 2

A. There are four types of snacks on this spinner.

B. The chances of winning a bag of popcorn are $\frac{1}{12}$.

C. You will probably get a free apple 10 times out of 30 spins.

D. You have the same chances of getting carrots as getting popcorn.

E. You have the smallest chance of getting pretzels.

Reproducible 17   *Chance Encounters*   ©EDC, 1994

Reproducible 17

Reproducible 17

▶ **From the Classroom**

One student explained a problem in game 1 like this: "Just read D and E. It says motorcycle and Rollerblades are both 50% and there's three more things."

▶ *Once students had identified the problems with the clues, I told them "Okay, designers, fix it!" Though students didn't always listen to each other, the groups found ways to work together.*

"All of the clues have to equal 100%," said Nick. "There's 93.75 left over."

"How did you figure that?" said Diego.

"You said $^1/_{16}$," said Nick, referring to a clue that had just been read.

"Don't change them to percents," said Diego. He then wrote the first clue: Lowest chance of getting bike.

"What about the car?" Nick asked. The boys turned to me and asked if they needed to include all items. I told them they could fix the clues any way they wanted to. "Let's demolish the car!" George declared, and the group agreed to leave out the car.

Their final version of the clues was:

1. Lowest chance of getting bike.

2. Skateboard has the same chance as bike.

3. You'll probably get motorcycle a quarter of the time.

4. 50% chance of getting Rollerblades.

Reproducible 18

2. Discussion: *What kinds of words and numbers can you use to write your own clues?*

In preparation for designing their own games, students brainstorm a list of ways to describe chances.

3. Investigation: *Design your own mystery spinner game.*

Design Your Own Mystery Spinner Games (Reproducible 18) provides guidelines for creating the games. Keeping the spinners to 3–5 parts helps ensure that the spinners can be described well in four clues.

This is a good activity to do in pairs; students often spark each other's creativity and can work together to solve the problems that arise in trying to make the spinner complete.

#18, Lesson 6

Design Your Own Mystery Spinner Game

Spinner Guidelines

- Draw a spinner with 3 – 5 parts.

- Label the spinner parts with the names of foods, music groups, sports, or whatever you want.

- Show the size of each spinner part by labeling it with a fraction or a percent.

Clue Guidelines

- Write at least 4 clues.

- Use a variety of words and numbers to describe the probability of spinning each spinner part.

- Make sure that your clues tell your classmates everything they need to know to draw your spinner.

Tip: Write your clues on a different piece of paper from your spinner. Keep the solution hidden from your classmates.

©EDC, 1995   *Chance Encounters*   *Reproducible 18*

Reproducible 18

For students who were having difficulty getting started, I suggested drawing the solution spinner first and then writing clues to describe it. This approach seemed to be easier than starting with the clues. Several students ran into problems because their solution spinners were labeled with incorrect fractions or percents or the parts didn't add up to 1. I encouraged students to check their spinners before moving on to writing the clues.

► *Some students wrote their clues as if they were describing graphs instead of spinners. For example, "Pizza is the most popular. Spaghetti is ¼ of the circle." I suggested that they imagine placing a transparent spinner over their drawing. Where would the arrow be most likely to land? I reminded them to describe the chances of each part of the spinner, such as "You have the best chances of getting pizza."*

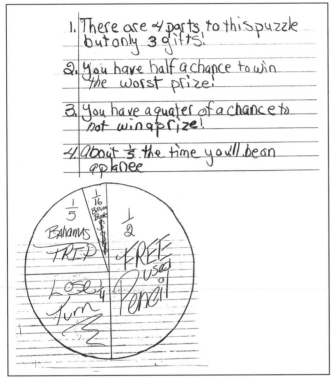

Spinner parts labeled incorrectly

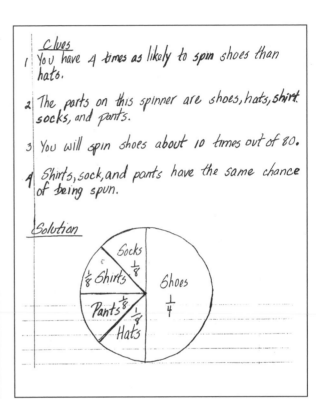

Clues are clearly written

4. Sharing: *Play your classmates' games and give them feedback.*

Students take on the role of game testers to try out and give feedback on a classmate's game.

TO THE STUDENT

Every game needs testing to make sure it works. Help a classmate test and revise his or her game.

- Exchange clues with a classmate. (Keep the solution spinner hidden.)
- Try to draw a spinner to match your classmate's clues.
- Give your classmate feedback on his or her game. Write answers to the following questions:
    1. What did you like about the game?
    2. What made the game easy or difficult to solve?
    3. Were the clues missing any information? If so, what information would you like to get from the clues?
    4. What suggestions would you like to give the designers?

Here are some tips for giving feedback:

- Remember, you are giving feedback in order to help someone else do a better job or to figure something out.
- Give feedback in a way that will help your classmates solve their problem, not make them feel bad.

Emphasize to students the importance of providing constructive feedback. You may want to give students some sample statements to complete, such as:

"I really like how you did . . ."

"Some things you could improve are . . ."

"I had trouble understanding what you meant by . . ."

"The part that seemed unclear to me was when you said . . ."

I wanted to play an active role in the feedback process so I had students put their clues on the blackboard and then had the whole class try to solve them together. We found that many of the games were missing information. Often, the game designers saw that something was wrong right after they wrote the clues up on the blackboard. I gave the designers the opportunity to fix the clues and then the class worked on finding a solution.

► *When my students tested each other's games, I was surprised to see many of them showed a sudden interest in fractions. Several of my students suggested that the designers use smaller fractions to make the mystery spinner games more challenging. "It was easy fractions . . . make the fractions harder." "One suggestion I would give to the designer is that he should add more parts." I couldn't believe it. They wanted to use fractions!*

> The game was kind of difficult to solve because the clues were confusing at first. Then after I read it over and over I understood the clues. I like the topic he chose.
>
> The game was easy because it was all in fractions, although the denominators were different, but easy to change. Most of the clues were given directly
>
> I thought the game was complicated which made it fun. I would suggest that in order to make it harder that they would need 10 types of sports. I liked their clues.

5. Writing: *Revise the games.*

Students read their classmates' feedback and examine the solutions that their classmates found. They then decide what changes to make to their game. Some games may have more than one solution.

You may want to use this activity as an assessment or as a homework option.

► **From the Classroom**

I emphasized that students did not have to use all the suggestions that were offered. It was up to them to decide how to change their games. Some students were surprised that their classmates drew a spinner that was different from their original one. I pointed out that some games might have multiple solutions. If students didn't want their game to have multiple solutions, they could try to add more clues or change the clues to ensure that only one spinner would match the clues.

6. Assessment: *Complete unfinished spinner games.*

Students apply what they've learned about designing spinner games to completing the problems on *Unfinished Games* (Reproducible 19). Students write clues for a given spinner and improve a game that has flawed clues.

ASSESSMENT CRITERIA

Do students' answers show that they understand how to:

- *Describe probabilities in a variety of ways (i.e., as fractions, percents, decimals, ratios).*

- *Interpret qualitative and quantitative descriptions of probabilities?*

- *Represent probabilities as parts of a circular spinner?*

- *Determine whether all the parts of a spinner add up to a whole?*

- *Use logical reasoning to solve problems?*

2) a: When you add up all the clues, it equals $2\frac{2}{3}$, and that doesn't even include basketball.

b:
* each of the clues has a name of a different sport: soccer, tennis, gymnastics, baseball & basketball

* tennis has a 1 in 3 chance of coming up.

* soccer and tennis have the same chances of coming up.

* Gymnastics has half as much chance of coming up as tennis.

* Baseball has half as much chance of coming up as Gymnastics

Good revision of clues

2 _Improve these clues_
a) The problem with these clues are that they add up to more than 100%. If tennis has $\frac{1}{3}$ chance of being spun, gymnastics will have two thirds chance of being spun because it says gymnastics has twice as much chance of coming up as tennis. Then it says baseball has twice as much chance of coming up as gymnastics So you can obviously see that this is over 100%.

b) _Clues_
1 The parts on the spinner are soccer, tennis, gymnastics baseball and basketball.

2 Tennis has 1 in 16 chance of coming up.

3 Soccer and tennis have the same chance of coming up.

4 Gymnastics has twice as much chance of coming up as tennis.

5 Baseball has 37.5% chance of coming up.

Clear explanation

7. Student Self-Assessment: *Reflecting on the spinner games.*

Students write about their experiences designing mystery spinner games and reflect on what they have learned in Section 2.

TO THE STUDENT

1. What do you like about the mystery spinner game you designed?
2. What would you do differently if you designed another mystery spinner game?
3. What does your game show about what you have learned so far in the unit?
4. What are some things that you have learned that your game doesn't show?

Homework Possibilities

Problem Solving

Have students draw at least four different qualitative spinners to describe the likelihood of real-world events.

Will I get to school on time?

Will I win the school raffle?

▶ *From the Classroom*

I loved this activity because my students' responses reflected their personalities and their senses of humor. Some of the real-world events they came up with: "I will be done with my morning shower before 7:00 a.m." "Any of us will ever be 10 again." "Whether a giant catfish will drink the entire Atlantic Ocean."

Writing

- What suggestions would you give your friends for designing Mystery Spinner Games?
- How can you check to make sure a game works?
- What makes a game easy or difficult to solve?

Software Possibilities

Students can use the *Chance Encounters* software to design a variety of spinners by specifying the probability of getting each part. Then they can run experiments with the spinners and compare the experimental and theoretical probabilities.

Answers

What's Wrong with This Game?

Game 1: It's impossible to draw a spinner to match the clues. If Rollerblades has a 50% chance of being spun, then it's not possible for bicycle to have the highest chance of being spun. Also, if Rollerblades and motorcycle have the same chances of being spun (50% and 50%), there wouldn't be any space left for the other parts. One way of fixing the clues is to change the probability of Rollerblades from 50% to 25%.

Game 2: The parts do not add up to a whole. Only about $\frac{1}{3}$ of the spinner is covered with parts. One way to fill up the rest of the spinner is to double the probabilities in the clues and change the probability of getting pretzels to $\frac{1}{3}$.

Unfinished Games

1. There are a variety of ways to describe the spinner. Students' clues should accurately describe the probabilities of the different parts.

2. Students' answers about what's wrong with the game should include some of the following points:
   a. The parts add up to more than 1 or 100%.
   b. Tennis and soccer are each $\frac{1}{3}$. That makes it impossible for gymnastics to be twice as likely as tennis.
   c. $\frac{2}{3}$ of the spinner is already full, so there's not enough space for another $\frac{2}{3}$.
   d. Similarly, it's impossible for baseball to be twice as likely as gymnastics.

   Students need to draw a solution spinner that will work and then write clues to describe it. The clues should accurately describe the probabilities in the solution spinner.

Fair and Unfair Games

In this section, students analyze and test the fairness of games involving two independent events, such as the tossing of two number cubes. Students analyze the rules of a game, make predictions about the game's fairness, and conduct experiments to test their predictions. They then create an outcome grid that shows the theoretical probabilities of all the possible outcomes in the game. As students compare games played with different rules and different combinations of game pieces, they explore the relationship between outcome grids, experimental data, and various numeric representations of probability.

The Game Fairness Lab in the optional *Chance Encounters* software provides a number of games students can test for fairness by having the computer quickly play the game a large number of times. Activities accompanying the software then challenge students to change the spinners of unfair games to make the games fair, and to change the spinners of fair games so that the players will have specified but unequal probabilities of winning.

Mathematical Themes

Theoretical and Experimental Probability

- Conduct probability experiments, including collecting, representing, and analyzing data.
- Determine all possible combinations of two independent events.
- Determine theoretical probabilities using outcome grids.
- Apply probability to determining fairness.
- Compare theoretical and experimental probabilities.
- Apply proportional reasoning to predict outcomes with large numbers of trials.

Approx. # of Classes	Lessons
2	**7. Is It Fair?** Students test the fairness of a number-cube game. They use an outcome grid to show all the possible outcomes and determine each player's probability of getting points.
2	**8. Charting the Chances: Exploring Outcome Grids** Students make outcome grids to analyze a variety of fair and unfair games.
2	**9. Which Game Would You Play?** Students represent probabilities as fractions, decimals, percents, and ratios. They compare the probabilities of winning different unfair games.

Lesson summary and sample schedule for Section 3

In this section, students explore more complex games in which the results depend on combining the outcomes of two game pieces. For example, in one game, player A receives a point when the sum of two spinner values is odd while player B receives a point when the sum is even. This raises an important question: How can you figure out all the possible combinations of two independent events and the probability of each combination?

Students learn to use an outcome grid to determine all possible combinations of two independent events. In an outcome grid, all the possible outcomes of one event are shown across the top and all the possible outcomes of the other event down the side. The boxes in the grid show the combinations.

Suppose you have one spinner divided into thirds, with the numbers 1–3, and another spinner divided into fourths, with the numbers 1–4, as shown below. In your game, you spin both spinners and add the two numbers. The grid below shows the possible sums, and the number of combinations that result in each sum. Since the spinners are divided into equal parts, each combination has the same probability of occurring.

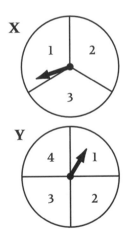

Numbers on Spinner Y

		1	2	3	4
Numbers on Spinner X	**1**	2	3	4	5
	2	3	4	5	6
	3	4	5	6	7

Suppose player A gets a point for each sum less than or equal to 3, while player B gets a point for each sum greater than 3. The outcome grid enables us to see that 3 out of 12 combinations give player A a point and 9 out of 12 combinations give player B a point.

As students make comparisons between experimental data and the outcome grid, they explore such questions as Does each player have an equal theoretical probability of winning? How many times is each player likely to win if you play a large number of times? Students apply the grid model to analyzing games with different combinations of game pieces. Using the grids, students investigate ways of changing the rules to make unfair games fair. For example, if the spinner game rules above are revised so that player A gets a point for a sum of 2, 3, or 4 and player B gets a point for a sum of 5, 6, or 7, then each player would have an equal probability of scoring a point.

In Lesson 9, student use outcome grids and proportional reasoning to make games fair by adjusting the rewards for winning. Students consider, for example, how the Carnival Games from Lesson 1 could be equalized by giving players different numbers of tickets for wins at different booths. If players are three times as likely to win tickets at booth A as they are at booth B, then the games can be made equal by awarding three times as many tickets for each win at booth B.

Multiple Representations of Probability

- Use visual models for analyzing theoretical probabilities.
- Explore numeric representations of probabilities and connect them with visual models.

Outcome grids are a visual model for analyzing and representing probabilities. They enable students to see all the possible outcomes of two independent events. By coloring or coding the grids, students get a clear picture of each player's probability of scoring points in a game.

Spinner Y

	1	2	3	4
1	2	3	4	5
2	3	4	5	6
3	4	5	6	7

Spinner X

■ Player A scores a point   ▨ Player B scores a point

In Lesson 9, students relate this model to fractions, decimals, percents, and ratios and apply these representations to comparing probabilities. Students come to understand the value of various numeric representations when they make comparisons between grids that show, for example, 4 favorable outcomes out of 9 and 7 favorable outcomes out of 15. In order to determine which game gives you the better chance of winning, students must represent the probabilities as percents or decimals. Later, students use the numeric representations to determine the expected number of points each player would receive in games with 100 or 1,000 turns.

Modeling Situations with Simulations

This section helps prepare students to analyze and create simulations in Section 4. Their comparisons of the theoretical and experimental probabilities in unfair games will enable students to test the accuracy of simulations. Students will also apply their understanding of outcome grids to design game boards for their own simulations of real-world events.

Teacher Reflections

"What Do You Mean by Luck?"

During our discussion of how students had revised the Special Sums Game, two students explained their methods for making the game fair. Tova had changed the rules so that each player had the same theoretical probability of winning ($^{12}/_{36}$). In contrast, Jake had changed the rules so that the players' probabilities were close but not equal ($^{10}/_{36}$, $^{12}/_{36}$, $^{14}/_{36}$). He still felt that the game was fair. As we compared the two games, the discussion moved from fairness to luck.

Some students decided that it didn't really matter which game they chose. Tomas: "[The probability that each player will win] doesn't have to be exactly the same. You don't know who will win or lose. It's luck." Anna: "Just because the players have the same chances, doesn't mean they'll get the same scores. Luck plays a big part." It seemed that some students were saying that it doesn't matter what the theoretical probability is because whether you win or lose will be determined by luck. Oh no, I thought, over halfway through the unit and some students are convinced that luck is responsible for whether a player wins or loses. After thinking about it for a moment, I wondered if that was really what students were saying, or was I so aware of the misconception students often have about luck that I was putting thoughts in their heads?

I decided to ask some clarifying questions. "I'm confused. You keep saying that whether someone wins or loses is all luck, so why do we even think about probability or how to make the games fair?"

"You can't predict a player's score in one game just because you know his chances of winning," said Anna. "It's unpredictable."

"It's unpredictable?" I asked, trying to push Anna's thinking.

"Yeah, you know," Anna answered, "the probability of getting heads is one out of two and you get tails on your first flip, then you might think you'll get heads on the second flip. Because the first flip out of two was a tails so the next flip has to be heads, right? It doesn't work that way, you can't predict it."

Once I had gotten Anna to move beyond the word *luck*, she articulated a pretty good definition of the concept of randomness. I wanted to see how well other students grasped the point, so I kept the discussion going. "So why do we talk about the probabilities of events then?"

"The probability is like what happens in general, or over a long time it will work out that way," said Sam. "If you try to test it with 10 flips, it may or may not match the probability. But if you do 100 or 1,000 flips, it will be really close to what the probability says."

"Yeah, it's like the average of something and it gives you a big general picture of something—like baseball statistics," said Raymond.

I felt much better after this discussion. Beyond students' casual references to luck lay a fairly sophisticated understanding of some big ideas, such as natural variability and the law of large numbers.

Teacher Reflections

Working with Outcome Grids

My students were able to "see" and read the outcome grid for the Special Sums Game quickly. They had no trouble finding the pattern or color-coding the outcomes. Many of the students commented that they had seen similar grids when they studied genetics in their science class. As a result, I was sure that they would breeze through the next lesson.

We started Lesson 8 the next day. As I walked around the room listening to groups of students make outcome grids, I was surprised by what I was hearing. Students were asking one another, "How do you make one of these things?" "How do you do it for a coin and a [digit] card?" "Why doesn't this come out right?" They sensed what a grid for two number cubes would look like, but they didn't know how to apply the model to games with other game pieces. I spent the rest of the class going from group to group helping them get started.

Students were having a variety of difficulties. Setting the grid up was a problem for many students. For example, they weren't sure what to put across the top of the grid or what to put down the left side. They didn't know how to figure out the total number of outcomes the game would have.

Similarly, some students thought that all grids should be square. They thought that there should be the same amount of numbers or letters across the top as down the side, like a grid for two number cubes or two coins. This made it difficult for them to set up grids for two different objects, such as a coin and a number cube.

Number Cube

Coin		1	2	3	4	5	6
	H	H1	H2	H3	H4	H5	H6
	T	T1	T2	T3	T4	T5	T6

Other students had assumed that all outcome grids followed a pattern because the grid for the Special Sums Game had a pattern. Students became confused when they couldn't see a pattern in the grid they were working on. Some students were so convinced that a grid must have a pattern that they created a pattern that had nothing to do with the outcomes.

This made me realize that the students were not as comfortable with grids as I had initially thought. I decided to take the time to review their grids. I asked each group to present a grid and explain it to the class. I was able to see if students were still having difficulties and offer assistance on the spot.

Lesson 7

Is It Fair?

How can you determine whether or not a game is fair? How can you change an unfair game to make it fair?

In this lesson, students use a theoretical model—an outcome grid—to evaluate the fairness of a number-cube game. Students make predictions and conduct experiments to test the game's fairness. After discovering that the game is unfair, students determine just how unfair it is by creating a grid that shows all the possible outcomes and each player's chances of winning the game. Like the spinners in Section 2, the outcome grids provide students with a strong visual model of probability. Students use the grids to create a version of the game that gives each player an equal chance of winning.

In Lesson 8, students use outcome grids to compare the fairness of various games.

Mathematical Goals

- Conduct probability experiments, including collecting, representing, and analyzing data.
- Determine all possible combinations of two independent events.
- Determine theoretical probabilities using outcome grids.
- Apply probability to determining fairness.
- Compare theoretical and experimental probabilities.

If I win, then the game is fair.

Materials

Per Student

Reproducible 22, *Change Special Sums*

Reproducible 23, *One Hundred Tosses*

Per Group of Three

Reproducible 20, *Is Special Sums Fair?*

Reproducible 21, *Making Outcome Grids*

Crayons or markers to color-code outcome grids

2 number cubes, preferably different colors (e.g., a red cube and a green one)

Per Class

Reproducible 21, *Making Outcome Grids* (transparency)

1. Investigation: *Is the Special Sums Game fair or unfair?*

Is Special Sums Fair? (Reproducible 20) provides the game rules and a format for testing the game for fairness. Introduce the game by playing a few rounds with the class and then have students record their predictions in Part 1 of the handout. Record the predictions for the whole class on the board so that they will be easy to compare to the game results.

Students play the Special Sums Game in groups of three. If some groups contain only two students, one student can be players A and C and the other, player B.

▶ From the Classroom

One student asked, "How can you get a sum of 1?" as soon as she read the rules. Another student responded "You can't! Unfair! Unfair!" That made other students eager to play the game and find other signs of unfairness. I held off discussing this further until after students had played the game.

▶ *Students had differing opinions on whether B or C had a better chance of winning. Some students thought that player C would win because he or she got points for the highest sums (9, 10, 11, 12). Others thought that player B would win because the sums (5, 6, 7, 8) would come up the most often.*

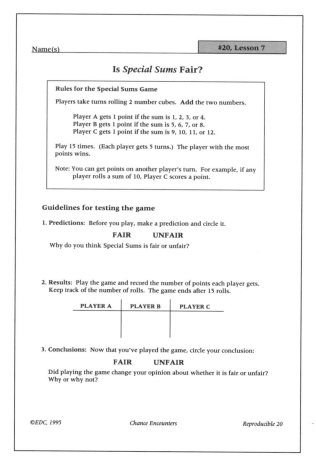

Reproducible 20

2. Discussion: *What do our results show about whether the game is fair or unfair?*

Make a graph or table of the class results and compare the results with the original predictions. One approach is to compare the number of games each player won rather than the number of points. The number of wins per player is easy to graph and it provides a dramatic picture of the unfairness of the game. An alternative approach is to compare the total and average points for each player, which is more time-consuming but provides more specific information about the game.

Here are some suggested questions to prompt discussion:

- How do the class results compare with the predictions?
- How do your group's results compare with the class results?
- Is the game fair or unfair? Why?
- If you played Special Sums 100 times, what do you think would happen? Why?

▶ **From the Classroom**

I asked each group which player won and recorded the data on a frequency graph.

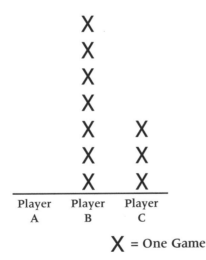

Results

Which player won each game?

X = One Game

▶ *In our class, player B won 6 of the games and player C won 1 game. Students seemed convinced that player A would never win, even in 100 games. When I asked if it was impossible for player A to win, Rebecca responded, "It's possible, but very unlikely."*

▶ *Karen explained that she thought the game was "unfair for A because there is no sum for 1, and for 2 there is only 1,1, and for 3 there is only 2,1, and for 4 there is 2,2 and 3,1, so there is less chances." Glenn agreed because "the small numbers are hard to get." This was a nice lead-in to the outcome grid.*

► **From the Classroom**

It took a while for students to understand what the grid was about. It helped to hold up two different-colored number cubes and show the box on the grid that would have that sum. For example, the sum of red 3 and green 4 is in a different box on the grid from the sum of green 4 and red 3.

► *I displayed the grid on the overhead projector and filled in two of the boxes. Slowly, students began telling me where to put different sums. Then they started to see patterns and talked about filling in whole diagonals with the same sum. I felt students got more out of discovering how to fill in the grid themselves than if I had led them through it.*

3. Problem Solving: *Use outcome grids to determine each player's chances of getting a point.*

Making Outcome Grids (Reproducible 21) shows students how to create a grid that provides a visual model of each player's theoretical probability of winning a point. Outcome grids can be used to figure out all the possible results for games involving two objects of chance that have equally likely parts, such as number cubes or coins, or two tosses of the same object.

Question 1 on the handout gets students thinking about the different ways to roll a sum with two number cubes. Emphasize to students the importance of looking at each cube individually: A roll of 1,2 is a different outcome from a roll of 2,1, even though both rolls equal the sum of 3. You may want to display the grid on an overhead projector and ask the class what numbers to put in each box.

Numbers on cube #1 (red)

	1	2	3	4	5	6
1	2					
2			5			
3						9
4						
5						
6						

Numbers on cube #2 (green)

Sum of the numbers on each cube

As students complete the grid, they start to see patterns emerge. Coloring the completed grids provides a strong visual model of the game's probabilities; students can easily compare the areas of the grid that correspond to each player's chances of winning points.

Red Cube (#1)

	1	2	3	4	5	6
1	2	3	4	5	6	7
2	3	4	5	6	7	8
3	4	5	6	7	8	9
4	5	6	7	8	9	10
5	6	7	8	9	10	11
6	7	8	9	10	11	12

Green Cube (#2)

■ Player A gets a point

□ Player B gets a point

■ Player C gets a point

4. Discussion: *How can you describe each player's chances of winning?*

Encourage students to analyze the kind of information provided by the grid:

- How many different outcomes does the game have?
- Which sum do you have the best chance of getting? the least chance?
- What are each player's chances of getting points?

This discussion provides a good opportunity to introduce the relationship between the outcome grid and numerical representations of probability. If no one suggests the following format, you may want to provide it to the class:

$$\frac{\text{Number of outcomes that give player A points}}{\text{Total number of outcomes}} = \frac{?}{?}$$

Sample Class Chart

Player A: 6 out of 36	6/36	1/6	.167	17%
Player B: 20 out of 36	20/36	5/9	.55	55%
Player C: 10 out of 36	10/36	5/18	.28	28%

You may also want to show the chances of each player's getting a point on a probability line.

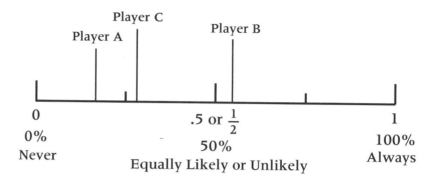

► **From the Classroom**

Students had different interpretations of what it means to make a game fair. Some students gave each player almost, but not exactly, the same chances of winning. For example, they gave player A 13 chances, B 12, and C 11. Dan, who had been player A, seemed to be looking for "revenge" and suggested that to make the game fair, player B should have less chances of winning. Jose explained that he had "tried to split [among the three players] the really hard ones like 2, 3, 11, and 12 that are almost impossible to get."

5. Problem Solving: *How can you make the game fair?*

Students change the rules of the Special Sums Game to make it fair. There are many ways to make the game fair, which can generate a good discussion of the definition of fairness: Does *fair* mean that players have exactly the same chance of winning? Students fill in and color one grid on *Change Special Sums* (Reproducible 22) to show that the revised rules make the game fair.

This activity works well for homework.

6. Extension: *Conduct an experiment with a large number of trials.*

Students conduct an experiment to see how many of each sum they might get if they roll two number cubes 100 times. *100 Tosses* (Reproducible 23) provides a format for conducting and analyzing the experiment. Students use their outcome grids from the Special Sums Game to predict which of the following bar graphs will match their results.

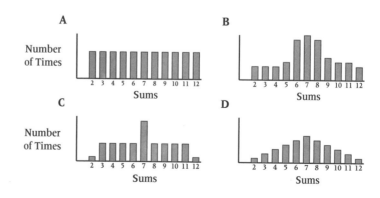

As students compare their results to their predictions, they gain a better understanding of the differences between experimental and theoretical probabilities.

Reproducible 23

I think the results were pretty surprising for me because I expected 6, 7, and 8 to stand out and have the most rolls. But instead there was a cluster in the middle which had about the same number of rolls. So nothing really stood out. But I have to say that 6 did stand out quite a bit on the bar graph.

I think my prediction of the graph was wrong because the graph I made for my experiment looks more like graph D. There is a midpoint. Then either side seems to slope.

I think the results would look pretty similar if I did 1000 turns. All the sums of tosses would probably be more concetrated in the center such as 6, 7, 8, and 9 because the more you roll the fewer exceptions you will have. It will balance out.

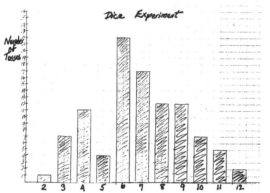

Homework Possibilities

Problem Solving

- *100 Tosses* (Reproducible 23) works well as homework. (Students need to have access to number cubes outside of class.)
- Students make Special Sums fair for four players. They write new rules and make a grid to show why the new version is fair.

Lesson 8

Charting the Chances: Exploring Outcome Grids

How can you use outcome grids to test the fairness of games involving coins, spinners, and digit cards as well as number cubes?

In this lesson, students design outcome grids to test the fairness of games of chance that have different numbers of outcomes. Students investigate games involving coins, spinners, digit cards, and number cubes in various combinations, which yield from 4 to 60 outcomes. In these game tests, unlike those in the previous lesson, students set up grids to match each game—including determining the number of possible outcomes. As they compare the outcome grids, students explore how the model can be adapted to represent probabilities in different kinds of games. The lesson ends with an assessment of students' understanding of outcome grids.

In Lesson 9, students make connections between the visual representations of outcome grids and different kinds of numeric representations.

Mathematical Goals

- Determine all possible combinations of two independent events.
- Use visual models to determine theoretical probabilities.
- Apply probability to determining fairness.

	Player B			
	1	2	3	4
Player A 1	2	3	4	5
2	3	4	5	6
3	4	5	6	7

Materials

Per Student	*Per Pair or Small Group*
Reproducible 25, *Perfect Products*	Reproducible 24, *Fair or Unfair?* (4 sheets)
Reproducible 26, *Sneaky Sums*	Large sheets of paper (for making outcome grids)
	Crayons or markers to color-code grids
	2 number cubes
	2 coins
	2 spinner transparencies
	10 digit cards (numbered 0–9)

Preparation

Make enough copies of *Fair or Unfair?* (Reproducible 24) so that each pair or small group of students can analyze at least one or two of the nine games. Students will need the rules and game pieces for only their assigned games.

Digit cards can be made by writing the numbers 0–9 on small index cards.

Suggested Lesson Plan

1. Investigation: *Are these games fair or unfair?*

Reproducible 24

The nine games on *Fair or Unfair?* (Reproducible 24) use spinners, number cubes, coins, digit cards, or combinations of two types of game pieces. The number of outcomes for the games range from 4 to 60. You may want to assign games to each pair of students or allow students to choose. It works well if the class as a whole covers a variety of games.

Since students will compare the grids for the different games later in the lesson, you may want them to make their outcome grids on large sheets of paper so that they can be displayed for the whole class to see.

An outcome grid for each of the games is provided at the end of the lesson.

TO THE STUDENT

Are these games fair or unfair? For each game:

- Predict whether the game is fair or unfair. If you think the game is unfair, which player do you think has the advantage?
- Play the game and record your results.
- Make an outcome grid for the game. Color or code the grid to show each player's probability of winning.
- Describe each player's probability of winning as a fraction, decimal, ratio, or percentage.
- Write your conclusions. Explain why the game is fair or unfair.

Note: Some of the games use two game pieces while others use one, such as a spinner spun twice. For games with one piece, one side of the outcome grid is for the first spin or toss and the other is for the second.

2. Discussion: *Compare the outcome grids for the different games.*

As students display and compare their grids, they see how the same model can be applied to different games. Here are some questions for discussing the grids:

- How did you figure out how many boxes to put in your outcome grid?
- Which games are fair? unfair? How can you tell?
- What are the similarities and differences among the grids for the games?
- What kinds of information can you get from an outcome grid?

3. Assessment: *Use an outcome grid to determine whether a game is fair or unfair.*

The problems on *Perfect Products* and *Sneaky Sums* (Reproducibles 25 and 26) give students the opportunity to demonstrate their understanding of outcome grids and probability. In the first part of the assessment, students make an outcome grid for a game and describe the players' probabilities of winning. In the second part, they are given a grid for a different game and they are asked to change the rules to make it fair.

Answers are provided at the end of the lesson.

Homework Possibilities

Problem Solving

Students choose one of the unfair games on *Fair or Unfair?* (Reproducible 24) and explore ways of making the game fair.

TO THE STUDENT

Make it fair!
1. Choose an unfair game that you have played.
2. Brainstorm ways of changing the game to make it fair.
   a. How could you change the rules for scoring points?
   b. How could you change the number of points each player gets?
   c. What other changes could you make?
3. Change the game to make it fair. (*Tip:* Don't make your changes too complicated. That will make it hard to show that your new version is fair.)
4. Explain why your new version is fair.

Writing

Dr. Math letters J and K (Appendix A).

Reproducibles 25 & 26

ASSESSMENT CRITERIA

Do students understand how to:

- *Make an outcome grid to show all the possible outcomes in a game?*
- *Describe each player's probability of winning in ratios, decimals, fractions, and percents?*
- *Determine whether a game is fair or unfair?*
- *Change the rules of an unfair game so that each player has an equal chance of winning?*

Software Possibilities

Students can use the *Chance Encounters* software to test games for fairness and to compare theoretical and experimental probabilities. With the software, students can quickly see what would happen if they played one of the games a large number of times. For example, they can simulate playing Special Sums 1,000 times and compare the number of points the three players get with their theoretical probabilities of getting points. Students can also experiment with changing the games by altering the number of parts and the values on the spinners. For example, students might explore the effects of making all the numbers odd or using spinners that have five parts instead of six. These investigations extend those in the lesson in which students change the rules of games while keeping the game pieces the same.

Answers

Fair or Unfair?

1. Match and Mismatch

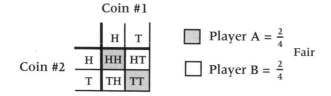

2. Two Heads are Better than One

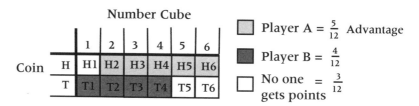

3. Odds and Evens Sums

Number Cube #2

Number Cube #1	1	2	3	4	5	6
1	2	3	4	5	6	7
2	3	4	5	6	7	8
3	4	5	6	7	8	9
4	5	6	7	8	9	10
5	6	7	8	9	10	11
6	7	8	9	10	11	12

Player A = $\frac{18}{36}$

Player B = $\frac{18}{36}$ Fair

4. Odds and Evens Products

Number Cube #2

Number Cube #1	1	2	3	4	5	6
1	1	2	3	4	5	6
2	2	4	6	8	10	12
3	3	6	9	12	15	18
4	4	8	12	16	20	24
5	5	10	15	20	25	30
6	6	12	18	24	30	36

Player A = $\frac{27}{36}$ Advantage

Player B = $\frac{9}{36}$

5. Spelling Bee

Spinner #2

Spinner #1	A	O	I	M
T	AT	TO	IT	TM
E	EA	OE	EI	ME
N	AN	ON	IN	NM
F	FA	OF	IF	FM

Player A = $\frac{9}{16}$ Advantage

Player B = $\frac{7}{16}$

6. Music Game

First Spin

Second Spin	Music Group 1	Music Group 2	Music Group 3	Radio 1	Radio 2
Music Group 1	C	B	B	A	A
Music Group 2	B	C	B	A	A
Music Group 3	B	B	C	A	A
Radio 1	A	A	A	C	B
Radio 2	A	A	A	B	C

Player A = $\frac{12}{25}$ Advantage

Player B = $\frac{8}{25}$

Player C = $\frac{5}{25}$

7. Hungry and Thirsty Game

Spinner

Coin	Beverage 1	Beverage 2	Food 1	Food 2	Food 3	Food 4	Food 5	Food 6
Heads	C	C	B	B	B	B	B	B
Tails	A	A	C	C	C	C	C	C

Player A = $\frac{2}{16}$

Player B = $\frac{6}{16}$

Player C = $\frac{8}{16}$ Advantage

8. Greater Than / Less Than

Digit Cards

Number Cube	0	1	2	3	4	5	6	7	8	9
1	10	11	21	31	41	51	61	71	81	91
2	20	21	22	32	42	52	62	72	82	92
3	30	31	32	33	43	53	63	73	83	93
4	40	41	42	43	44	54	64	74	84	94
5	50	51	52	53	54	55	65	75	85	95
6	60	61	62	63	64	65	66	76	86	96

Player A = $\frac{12}{60}$

Player B = $\frac{18}{60}$

Player C = $\frac{30}{60}$

9. What's the Difference Game

Even Digit Cards

	0	2	4	6	8
1	1	1	3	5	7
3	3	1	1	3	5
5	5	3	1	1	3
7	7	5	3	1	1
9	9	7	5	3	1

Odd Digit Cards (row labels)

Player A = $\frac{9}{25}$

Player B = $\frac{8}{25}$

Player C = $\frac{8}{25}$

Perfect Products

Probability of getting a point:

Player A: $\frac{8}{24}$	.33	33%	8 out of 24	1 out of 3
Player B: $\frac{6}{24}$	.25	25%	6 out of 24	1 out of 4
Player C: $\frac{7}{24}$	.29	29%	7 out of 24	
Player D: $\frac{3}{24}$	.125	13%	3 out of 24	1 out of 8

	0	1	2	3	4	5
3	0	3	6	9	12	15
4	0	4	8	12	16	20
3	0	5	10	15	20	25
4	0	6	12	18	24	30

Player A   Player B

Player C   Player D

Sneaky Sums

Two ways of changing the rules are:

1. Player A gets 1 point when the sum is 5, 6, or 8.

   Player B gets 1 point when the sum is 4, 7, or 9.

   Player C gets 1 point when the sum is 10, 11, 12, or 13.

2. Player A gets 1 point when the sum is 4, 9, 11, or 13.

   Player B gets 1 point when the sum is 5, 7, or 10.

   Player C gets 1 point when the sum is 6, 8, or 12.

Each player's probability of getting a point is $\frac{10}{30}$ or $\frac{1}{3}$ or .33 or 33%.

Lesson 9

Which Game Would You Play?

How can fractions, decimals, percents, and ratios help you compare the chances of winning games with different numbers of outcomes?

Students use numerical representations of probabilities to rank the chances of winning at different games. Students begin by coloring 36-box grids to represent probabilities expressed as fractions, percents, ratios, and decimals. They move on to apply their knowledge of numerical representations to comparing and ranking grids for games with different numbers of outcomes. As students translate the grids into fractions, percents, ratios, and decimals, they discover how numerical expressions can be useful for comparing probabilities. Students then create an outcome grid to compare the chances each player has of winning a game in which different outcomes result in different numbers of points.

Mathematical Goals

- Explore numeric representations of probabilities and connect them with visual models.
- Develop a sense of the relative size of different probabilities.
- Recognize that when working with probabilities the number of favorable outcomes needs to be considered in proportion to the total number of outcomes.
- Apply proportional reasoning to predict outcomes with large numbers of trials.

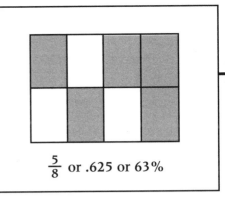

$\frac{5}{8}$ or .625 or 63%

Materials

Per Student	**Per Pair**	**Per Class**
Reproducible 27, *From Numbers to Grids*	Reproducible 29, *Is This High-Scoring Game Fair?*	Reproducible 27, *From Numbers to Grids* (optional transparency)
Reproducible 28, *Rank the Grids*		Reproducible 28, *Rank the Grids* (optional transparency)
Reproducible 30, *Back to the Carnival*		
Reproducible 2, *Carnival Games*		
Calculator (optional)		

Suggested Lesson Plan

1. Problem Solving: *Compare the probabilities of winning unfair games.*

From Numbers to Grids (Reproducible 27) introduces a process for comparing the chances of winning different unfair games. Students fill in 36-box grids to correspond with different kinds of numerical representations of probability (for example, $^{16}/_{36}$ and 25%).

    After students complete their grids, you may want to use these questions for discussion:

- How did you figure out how many boxes to fill in?
- How did you rank the grids from best to worst chances of winning?
- How would you show the probabilities on a grid that had 72 boxes?

> Reproducible 27

▶ From the Classroom

My students found it hard to get started when the probability was listed in something other than 36ths. After a few minutes, though, the class came up with a lot of different strategies. One student who was trying to shade 25% of the grid covered half the grid with her hand and said, "That's 50%." She then covered half of the remaining 50% and said, "That's 25%." Once she had broken it down, she was able to color in 25% of the grid. Another student set up equivalent fractions without knowing that was what he was doing. He was trying to shade 6/18ths of the grid. He explained to me that if he doubled 18 he would get 36 so if he doubled 6 then he would know how many he would have to color.

2. Problem Solving: *Which grids show the best chances of winning?*

In *Rank the Grids* (Reproducible 28), students find two different numerical representations of the player's probability of winning each game. They then rank the probabilities from best to worst chances of winning.

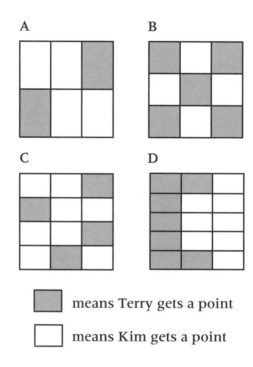

■ means Terry gets a point

☐ means Kim gets a point

Unlike the 36-box grids students worked with in Step 1, the grids on *Rank the Grids* have different numbers of boxes. Since the grids cannot be compared by counting, students see the value in using fractions, decimals, percents, or ratios to compare and rank the games.

Answers are provided at the end of the lesson.

3. Discussion: *How did you figure out which game would be best for Terry? How many points do you think Terry would get if she played that game 100 times?*

Students share their strategies for ranking the games and make connections between theoretical and experimental probabilities. They use the theoretical probabilities to predict how many points each player would be likely to get if they played each game 100 times.

Some questions for discussion:

- How did you rank the probabilities of winning the games?
- How did you make a grid that is better for Terry than the second-best game but not as good as the best game? Is there more than one possible grid?
- For each game, how many points do you think Terry would be likely to get in 100 turns? How many points would Kim be likely to get?
- Terry and Kim had a marathon and played one of the games 500 times. Their scores were Terry, 235 points and Kim, 265 points. Which game do you think they played? Why?

2. I made the number of black squares into percentages. I did it by making the grids into fractions then into decimals then percents.

④

$\left(\frac{15}{32}\right)$

.46875

4. Investigation: *How can you determine the fairness of games in which players score different numbers of points?*

In *Is This High-Scoring Game Fair?* (Reproducible 29), students use proportional reasoning and outcome grids to explore the relationship between the probabilities and number of points that each player can score. This activity gives students the opportunity to apply and extend their understanding of outcome grids and numeric representations of probabilities.

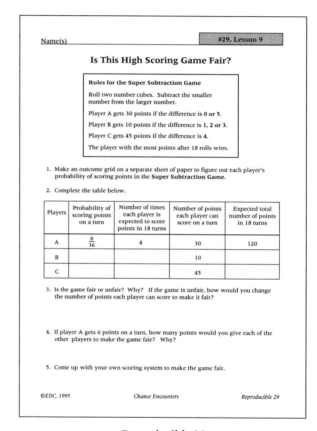

Reproducible 29

In questions 3, 4, and 5 on the reproducible, students change the scoring system for the game to make it fair. By changing the number of points each player can get for winning a turn, students are equalizing the number of points each player is likely to get over the course of several turns. For example, if A is likely to score on 50 out of 100 turns and B on 25 out of 100, then you can equalize the number of points if B can score 2 points on a turn while A can only score 1. The term for describing the combination of the probabililty of winning a turn and the amount of points scored per turn is *expected value*.

Answers are provided at the end of the lesson.

5. Problem Solving: *What are the probabilities of winning the different carnival games?*

The problems on *Back to the Carnival* (Reproducible 30) give students the opportunity to apply what they've learned in Sections 2 and 3 to the Carnival Games from Lesson 1. Their knowledge of outcome grids enables them to analyze the chances of winning in the Coin and Cube and Teens Only games.

Homework Possibilities

Writing

Dr. Math letters L and M (Appendix A).

Problem Solving

- *Back to the Carnival* (Reproducible 29) works well as homework.
- Long-term assignment: Review a game.

Reproducible 30

ASSESSMENT CRITERIA

Do students understand how to:

- *Figure out theoretical probabilities by using outcome grids?*
- *Represent probabilities as fractions, decimals, ratios, or percents?*
- *Rank probabilities on a scale of 0–1?*

TO THE STUDENT

- Choose a game to research. (Choose a game of chance that you like a lot or one that you have never played. You may want to pick a game from another country.)
- Write a review of the game to tell your classmates all about it. Here are some questions to answer in your review:
  1. What is the game about? How do you play?
  2. What country is the game from?
  3. How does the game involve chance? making choices? physical skill?
  4. What kind of game pieces does the game use? What are the possible outcomes? What are the probabilities of the outcomes?
  5. If the game has a board, what are the probabilities of landing on different types of boxes?
  6. Is the game fair? Why or why not?
  7. What do you like about the game?
  8. Is there anything you dislike about the game?
  9. Who would you recommend the game to?

You may want students to investigate games from countries that they are studying in social studies. The table on page 95 lists some games from around the world, many of which were developed hundreds of years ago. See Sources for Further Information for a list of books that contain the rules for these and other games. Some of the games are available from NCTM.

Software Possibilities

The optional *Chance Encounters* software has six games for students to investigate and compare. With the software, students can play each game a large number of times and then use the results to rank the games from best chances of winning to worst chances for a particular player. In addition, students can change the spinners to increase or decrease a player's probability of winning.

Answers

From Numbers to Grids

Ranked from best to worst (best = 1): C, 1; E, 2; A, 3; D and F, 4; B, 5

Probability of *not* winning:
A: $^{20}/_{36}$
B: 75%
C: 1 out of 4
D: $^{2}/_{3}$
E: .50
F: 12 out of 18

Rank the Grids

1. Descriptions of Terry's chances of winning.
    A: $^{2}/_{6}$, .33, 33%
    B: $^{5}/_{9}$; .56; 56%
    C: $^{4}/_{12}$; .33; 33%
    D: $^{7}/_{15}$; .47; 47%
2. Ranked from best to worst (best = 1): B, 1; D, 2; A and C, 3
3. Answers will vary.
4. Any grid with a probability greater than .47 and less than .56. For example, 12 boxes with 6 shaded.

Games	Origins	Game Pieces
All-tes-teg-enuk	North America (Native American game)	Six thin stones, plain on one side and colored on the other
Chausar	India	4-sided dice (sides have one, two, five, and six dots)
Goose	Italy	2 dice
Ka-wa-su-suts	United States (New Mexico)	3 sticks, decorated with 2,3, or 10 bands
Life	United States	Spinner
Lu-Lu	United States (Hawaii)	Four round discs of volcanic stone about 2.5 cm in diameter; the stones are plain on one side and the other side is marked with 1,2,3, or 4 dots
Pachisi	India	Original version: cowrie shells; Modern version: dice
Patolli	Aztec	5 large beans (called patolli) with a hole drilled on one side to form a white dot
Senet	Egypt	4 casting sticks
Shut the Box	France, Zambia	2 dice
Snakes and Ladders	India, England	1 or 2 dice
Totolopsi	North America (Native American game)	3 sticks, each having one face flat and the other curved and marked with a pattern of dots
T'shu-p'u	China	2 four-sided dice marked 1, 6, 3, and 4
Ur	Sumerian City of Ur	3 pyramid-shaped dice; each has two of its tips marked
Yahtzee	United States	4 dice

Cube #1

	1	2	3	4	5	6
1	0	1	2	3	4	5
2	1	0	1	2	3	4
3	2	1	0	1	2	3
4	3	2	1	0	1	2
5	4	3	2	1	0	1
6	5	4	3	2	1	0

Cube #2

Player A = $\frac{8}{36}$

Player B = $\frac{24}{36}$

Player C = $\frac{4}{36}$

Is This High-Scoring Game Fair?

2. Completed table:

Players	Probability of scoring points on a turn	Number of times each player is expected to score points in 18 turns	Number of points each player can score on a turn	Expected total number of points in 18 turns
A	8/36	4	30	120
B	24/36	12	10	120
C	4/36	2	45	90

3. The Super Subtraction Game is unfair because the expected value of points for player C is lower than that for players A and B. If the number of points player C can score on a turn is changed to 60, then the game will be fair.

4. A: 6 points; B: 2 points; C: 12 points.

5. Answers will vary.

Back to the Carnival

1. Chances of winning:

   Outcome grid for Coin and Cube booth:

Number Cube

Coin		1	2	3	4	5	6
	H	H1	H2	H3	H4	H5	H6
	T	T1	T2	T3	T4	T5	T6

Win 1 ticket, probability is $\frac{4}{12}$

0 tickets, probability is $\frac{8}{12}$

Outcome grid for Teens Only booth:

Second Toss

First Toss	1	2	3	4	5	6
1	11	12	13	14	15	16
2	12	22	23	24	25	26
3	13	23	33	34	35	36
4	14	24	34	44	45	46
5	15	25	35	45	55	56
6	16	26	36	34	56	66

(shaded) Win 1 ticket, probability is $\frac{8}{36}$

(unshaded) 0 tickets, probability is $\frac{28}{36}$

2. Probability line:

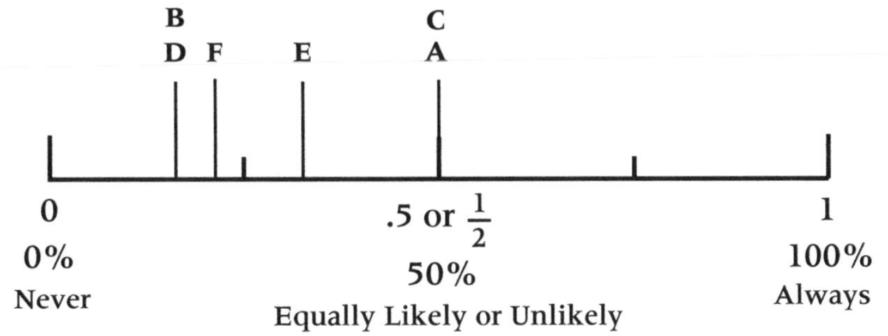

B
D F E
C
A
0
0%
Never
.5 or $\frac{1}{2}$
50%
Equally Likely or Unlikely
1
100%
Always

3. Completed table:

Booth	*Theoretical Probability of Winning on 1 Turn*	*Expected No. of Wins in 12 Turns*	*Number of Tickets You Can Win on a Turn*	*Expected Total Number of Tickets in 12 Turns*
A. Get Ahead	1/2	6	4	24
B. Lucky 3s	1/6	2	12	24
C. Evens and Odds	1/2	6	4	24
D. Pick a Number	1/6	2	12	24
E. Coin and Cube	1/3	4	6	24
F. Teens Only	8/36	2.64	9	23.76

Simulations: Using Probability to Model Real-World Events

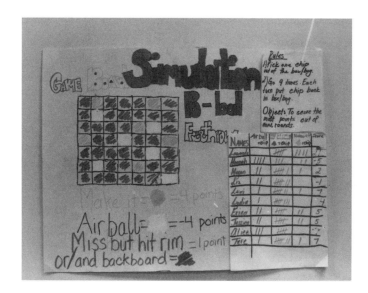

Many games are designed to simulate things people really do. Students may be familiar with board, card, or video games that simulate playing a sport, flying a plane, running a business, planning a city, traveling around the world, or any number of other activities. Each of these games captures, in simplified form, some of the events in the actual activity and the probabilities of those events.

In this section, students test the realism of a simulation by playing the game and comparing their results to data from the actual activity. Do the probabilities of events in the simulation reflect the probabilities in its real-world counterpart? After testing a simulation in which real-world data are provided, students move on to collect their own data for a simple game of skill and use it to create a number-cube simulation of the game. This activity helps prepare students for the final project, in which they collect data and design a simulation for an activity of their choice. The unit ends with presentations and assessment of the final projects.

Approx. # of Classes	Lessons
2	**10. Is It Realistic? Testing Simulations** Students test simulation games that are played with a grid and two number cubes. They determine how realistic the games are by comparing data from playing the simulations with data from the actual sports.
2	**11. Simulating a Simple Game** Students collect data on a game of skill and then create a simulation to match their game results.
3+*	**12. Final Project: Design Your Own Simulation Game** Students design a simulation of an activity that they know well. They collect and analyze data, make a probability line, design an outcome-grid game board, and test their simulations.
1–2	**13. Project Seminar: Testing the Simulations** Students present their simulation games and play them.

Lesson summary and sample schedule for Section 4

Mathematical Themes

Theoretical and Experimental Probability

- Collect and analyze data to determine the probabilities of real-world events.
- Conduct experiments to determine probabilities.
- Use grid models to represent and analyze theoretical probabilities.

The core of simulating a situation is to build a game with theoretical probabilities that match—as closely as possible—the experimental probabilities for the events that can happen in the situation. This is described further under Modeling Situations with Simulations. To create and test simulations, students use the techniques for conducting probability experiments and the techniques for analyzing theoretical probabilities that they developed in Sections 1, 2, and 3.

Multiple Representations of Probability

- Represent probability verbally, visually, and numerically.

In this section, students use the representations they have developed throughout Sections 1, 2, and 3 to represent both experimental and theoretical probabilities. Probability lines, outcome grids, numeric representations, and verbal descriptions are all used in the process of testing and creating simulations. These representations enable students to compare probabilities in the simulations with those in the actual activity.

Modeling Situations with Simulations

- Model the probabilities of real-world events by creating simulations.
- Test simulations by comparing the probabilities of events in a simulation and its real-world counterpart.
- Apply probability and statistics to making simulations more realistic.

The process of creating a simulation begins with collecting data about the frequency of the different events in the actual activity. For example, if the simulation is about baseball, we would need data about the number of at-bats that result in singles, doubles, triples, home runs, outs, and whatever other events from baseball we want to include in the simulation. We then need to use this statistical data to determine the probabilities of the different events.

The goal of creating the simulation is to make the theoretical probabilities within the simulation reflect the experimental probabilities of the actual events. For example, if the baseball data show that players hit singles in about 20% of their at-bats, then a single should occur with about this same frequency in the simulation. This can be done by using a 36-box grid and labeling 7 of the boxes single (see Figure 1). The most likely event in the actual sport should have the highest probability of happening in the simulation and the least likely event should have the lowest.

Testing and creating simulations raise many questions about statistics and probability. Students must consider the population from which the statistical data were obtained: Does the baseball simulation pertain to middle school softball games or professional baseball games? Students must consider both the average and range of outcomes: Does the baseball simulation result in a reasonable highest score, lowest score, and average score? They must also consider the law of large numbers and the quantity of data required to provide a good test of a simulation.

Baseball Grid
Cube #1 (Red)

	1	2	3	4	5	6
1	Single	Single	Single	Single	Single	Single
2	Single					
3						
4						
5						
6						

Cube #2 (Green)

Figure 7.

When the students had finished playing the miniature golf simulation, we made frequency graphs of their results. Then we compared our results to the real-world scores. When the students saw that the real-world scores were lower than ours, they decided that the simulation needed revision.

This is the point where I got stuck! I was confused about how to translate the real-world data so that they could revise the simulation. Finally, I told the class, "This isn't working!" I apologized for not knowing what to do and admitted that I wasn't explaining the process to them correctly. "So what!" said one of the students. "Let's try to figure it out!" I was grateful for the encouragement and decided that this could be a good opportunity to show students how to problem-solve.

As the class began studying the real-world data, it occurred to me that it would be easier for the students to work with the data if we focused on the averages. This way students could get a picture of what was likely to happen in a game (18 holes). For example, in an average game, a player would get about 11 holes in 2 strokes and 4 holes in 3 strokes. Since all the averages were in terms of 18 holes, students could double them to figure out how many boxes to give each event on a 36-box grid. I made a table for the class to complete:

Event	Average Times per Game (18 holes)	Number of Boxes on a 36-Box Grid
Hole-In-One	1.9	4
2 Strokes	11.1	22
3 Strokes	3.7	8
4 Strokes	1.1	2
5 Strokes	.09	0

It worked beautifully and I was impressed with the students' patience and understanding. I think it was good for them to see that sometimes things get complicated and you need to step back and approach it in a different manner. To me, that was a great mathematics lesson.

Teacher Reflections

Sharing the Final Projects

On the day the projects were due, my students came in with very elaborate, colorful, simulation game boards and an endless supply of enthusiasm. They were really eager to have their games played, and to play their classmates' games.

I asked the class to help me create a system for testing the simulation games. Did they want to move from game to game in pairs? How many games did they each want to play? They were very quick to reject anything so formal. "Can't we just play the games we want to play?" "Can't we choose who we want to play with?" They had worked really hard on their projects, and as far as I was concerned, this was their day. So I let them choose how they wanted to work and with whom. After the games were set up, I placed a stack of testing sheets next to each one for students to fill out. I wanted them to give each other feedback on the simulations.

They had a terrific time playing each other's games. Most of them chose to work with the same pair or group of three students. Some roamed around the room, alone or with a friend, and tried out different games. When I stood back and watched what was going on in my room, I noticed it had the feeling of a carnival. This seemed like a perfect way to end the unit. We started the unit with the carnival games and ended with our own carnival, with the students' games as the various booths.

I was really impressed with the range, including basketball, baseball, soccer, Monopoly, an invented bowling-like game, toss-the-ball-in-a-cup, pro tennis, walking a dog, traffic jam, sailing, skateboarding, "scurf boarding," snowboarding, and dancing. Their games also used an assortment of playing pieces, including colored chips, spinners, and number cubes. The variety and appeal of their games added to the carnival-like atmosphere.

At one table, three boys were having a terrific time playing one another's games. They decided to act out the various events in the simulations, for example, pretending to do a 360-degree spin during Jason's simulation of skateboarding. They even added a rule to Matthew's game, "You can act it out if you want." When they were finished, they wrote on the testing sheet, "We learned three things—probability, acting, and subtracting." I overheard one of the boys say, "This is cool!" I was thrilled to hear that in my math class.

At this point in the unit, given how much effort they had given and how much they had learned, I would have been happy if this was strictly a fun period for them. As a real bonus for me, though, I noticed that students were really thinking about the games as they played, and taking the testing sheets seriously. They were thoughtfully giving oral feedback to the game designers and writing their comments on the testing sheets. Some students were revising their games as they played and discovered problems. Others would be able to go away with a stack of completed testing sheets to help them reflect on their projects.

It was obvious that my students were very proud of their games. So was I. I had set high expectations for their final projects, and encouraged them to make their games "spectacular," and they did.

Lesson 10

Is It Realistic? Testing Simulations

How can you determine whether a game is a realistic simulation of a sport?

Students investigate the realism of a simple simulation of either baseball or miniature golf. The simulations are played by rolling two number cubes: each combination of outcomes corresponds to an event such as getting a hole in one or a home run. Students collect data to determine the probability of events in the simulation and then compare their results to statistics from the actual sport. They analyze the two sets of data to answer questions like Are you more likely to get a home run in the simulation or the actual sport? Are the scores from the simulation consistent with those of people actually playing miniature golf? As a final step, students revise the simulation to make it more realistic.

In Lessons 11 and 12, students design and test their own simulations.

Mathematical Goals

- Use experiments to determine the probabilities of events in a simulation.
- Analyze data to determine the probabilities of real-world events.
- Use averages to compare sets of data.
- Test whether the frequency of events in a simulation accurately reflects the frequency of events in its real-world counterpart.
- Apply probability and statistics to making a simulation more realistic.

Materials

Per Student	Per Pair or Small Group	Per Class
Calculators (optional)	One of the following pairs of sheets:	One of the following:

Per Pair or Small Group (continued):

Reproducible 31, *Simulation Miniature Golf*/Reproducible 32, *Miniature Golf Scoresheet*

Reproducible 33, *Simulation Baseball*

Reproducible 34, *Baseball Scorecard*

2 number cubes, each of a different color

Per Class (continued):

Reproducible 35, *Miniature Golf Actual Data* (transparency)

Reproducible 36, *Baseball Actual Data* (transparency)

Sheets of chart paper for making class graphs

Preparation

Two simulations are provided with this lesson: miniature golf and baseball. It is best to have the entire class do the same simulation, so there will be sufficient data to compare with the data provided about the actual activity.

Miniature golf is a good option because the game is simple to explain and the number-cube simulation is easy to play. It also works particularly well because there are 18 holes in a game and 36 boxes in the grid; students can count the average number of times each outcome occurs in a game and double it to figure out how to fill in the grid.

Number-cube baseball is slightly more complex because students need to read the grid and then move players around on a baseball diamond. Also, the number of at-bats may vary in each of the nine innings.

Suggested Lesson Plan

1. Introduction: *What games are designed to be like a real sport or other activity?*

Introduce the concept of and term *simulation*. Within the context of this unit, a simulation is a game designed to be similar to a real activity. The events in a simulation should be among those that occur in the real activity, and the likelihood of the different events in the simulation should correspond to that in the real activity.

Students will probably begin naming games that simulate sports, but they may also be familiar with games that simulate running a business, being a detective, or other types of activities. They may know board games and video games that are simulations, and they may have created their own simple simulations, such as versions of football or soccer that can be played on the lunchroom table.

2. Investigation: *Testing a simulation game.*

The memo on page 107 introduces the task of testing a simulation game and outlines the steps students will carry out in this lesson.

Reproducibles 31–32 or 33–34

▶ **From the Classroom**

I asked students who were familiar with miniature golf to explain the game to their classmates. One student acted out playing the game to explain why low scores were better than high scores.

MEMO 2

To: Apprentice Game Designers
From: Designers of New Products

We're developing new simulation games.
The great thing about these simulations is
that you can play the sports at your desk
just by rolling two number cubes. You'll
get holes in one, home runs, and strike-
outs just like in the real games. Your scores
will be just like the scores of real players.

Your assignment is to test a simulation
game to see how realistic it is. To test a
simulation, you will need to:

- Play the simulation to collect data about
  how often each event in the simulation
  occurs.

- Analyze data to find out how often each
  event happens in the real sport.

- Compare your results from the simulation to what happens in the actual
  sport.

- Make recommendations about how to
  change the simulation in order to make
  it more realistic.

Demonstrate how to play a simulation by displaying the grid
on an overhead and playing a few turns. (Have students
change the colors on the grid—blue and red—to correspond to
the colors of the number cubes they are using.) The picture on
page 108 shows how to read the golf grid. The baseball grid is
read in the same way.

The simulations are intentionally flawed so that the probabilities of events do not accurately reflect the probabilities in
the actual sport. Background information on the simulations is
provided at the end of the lesson.

3. Data Collection: *How often do the different events occur in the simulation game?*

Students play the simulation in pairs or small groups. Before
they begin, you may want students to predict how often they
think the best event (e.g., hole in one, home run) will happen
when they play. They can figure out the theoretical probability
from the grid. After playing, students combine their data to
make frequency graphs or tables so that they can compare the

How to Play the Miniature Golf Simulation

No. of Players: 2-4

Materials: 2 different colored number cubes and a game grid.

How to read the game grid: If you roll a 4 on the red cube and a 2 on the yellow cube you will get a "Good Shot" and score 2 points. That means it took you only 2 tries to get the ball in the hole.

Red / Yellow	1	2	3	4	5	6
1	Hole in One (1)	Missed by a Mile (5)	Putt, Putt Putt (3)	In the Water (4)	Out of Control (5)	Lost Your Touch (4)
2	Wimpy Putt (3)	Hole in One! (1)	Wimpy Putt (3)	Good Shot! (2)	Perfect Putt (2)	Putt, Putt Putt (3)

Rules: Players alternate taking turns. On your turn, roll the number cubes to find out how many tries it took to get the ball in the hole. The player with the *least* number of points after 18 holes wins.

In miniature golf, low scores are better than high scores.

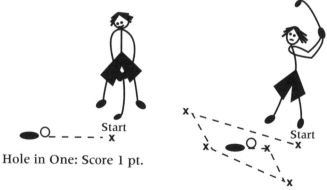

Hole in One: Score 1 pt.

Five tries to get ball in hole: Score 5 pts.

number of times each event happened. You may want to post a sheet of chart paper for each event and have students add their data to the graphs.

Divide the class into small groups and give each one a frequency graph for a different event. Each group calculates the average number of times the event occurred and reports their findings to the class. In Step 4, students will compare the averages from the simulation to those from the actual sport. For the miniature golf simulation, students can also compare the total scores and average scores with those from actual players. For baseball, they can compare the average number of runs per game to the actual average. The figures below show the results from the miniature golf simulation game for one class:

Our Scores in the Mini Golf Simulation

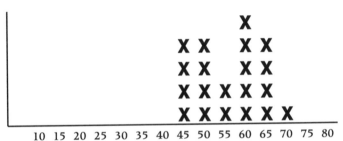

Number of Holes in One Scored by Each Student

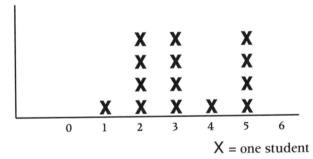

X = one student

Some questions for analyzing the results include:

• How do your results compare with your classmates'?
• How often did the best event and the worst event occur? How do these results compare with the theoretical probabilities for those events?
• What is the average score? What is the average number of times each event occurred?

Reproducible 35 or 36

4. Discussion: *How does the data from the simulation compare with the actual data?*

Display the data from the actual sport (Reproducible 35 or 36) on an overhead so that students can check the accuracy of the simulation. Students can compare their class averages from the simulation to those from the actual sport. They may also want to calculate experimental probabilities for the events, which can be done by using either the averages or the total occurrences. For example, the experimental probability for getting 2 strokes in an average game is the ratio of 11.1 (the average times per game) to 18 (the number of holes in a game), which equals 62%. Alternatively, the ratio of 477 (the total occurrences in 43 games) to 774 (the total number of holes played) also equals 62%.

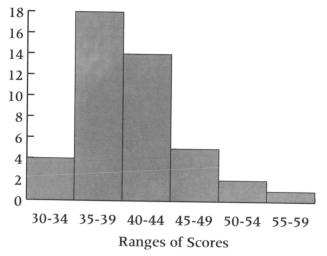

Graph of Scores in 43 Actual Mini-Golf Games

Here are some sample questions to help students compare the data:

- Does the best event happen more often in the simulation or in the actual sport? For example, are you more likely to get a home run in the simulation or in a real baseball game?
- Use the actual data to rank the events from most likely to least likely to occur. How does that compare with the results of playing the simulation?
- How do the averages for the events in the simulation compare with the averages in the actual sport?

5. Investigation: *How would you revise the simulation to make it more realistic?*

The process of revising the game helps students gain a better understanding of how these simulations work and prepares them for designing their own simulation in the final project. This activity can be done individually or in pairs and works well as homework.

TO THE STUDENT

Using the data you've collected, revise the simulation to make it more realistic.

- Make a new grid for the simulation. How many boxes do you want to give each event?
- Describe how you decided what changes to make.

There are different approaches to making the simulation more realistic. Students can divide the 36 boxes of the grid among the events so that they are in proportion to the averages from the actual data. For example, fly or ground out (avg. 19.52) might get 20 boxes while strikeout (avg. 5.31) would get 5 boxes. For the minigolf simulation, students can double the averages (for 18 holes) to figure out the number of boxes on the 36-box grid. An alternative approach is to figure out the experimental probability of each event and then multiply it by 36. For example, in the golf game, getting a hole in 2 strokes has a probability of 62%. Multiplying 62% by 36 equals about 22, so there should be about 22 boxes with the outcome.

In baseball, students can find the experimental probabilities by dividing the number of times an event occurred by the total number of at-bats (5,579). With this method, students will find that getting a triple has such a low probability of happening that it would not get a box on the grid. However, since it is an event in the actual sport, students may still want to include it and reduce the number of boxes for another event.

Homework Possibilities

Problem Solving

- Revising the simulation to make it more realistic (Step 5) works well as homework.
- Students test the simulation not worked on in class.

Some students suggested cutting the scores of 4 and 5 strokes from the miniature golf simulation. Other students thought that would make the simulation less realistic and less exciting to play: "When I play miniature golf, I get a lot of 4s and 5s." "If everyone always gets a good score, it's not as much fun." Students decided that the simulation should have fewer 4s and 5s than the original one but a higher percentage than the real-world data. The chances of getting 5s in the simulation went from 7 out of 36 (14%) to 1 out of 36 (3%) and 4s went from 6 out of 36 (17%) to 3 out of 36 (8%).

ASSESSMENT CRITERIA

Do students' revised games show that they understand:

- *How to analyze data to determine the relative frequency of events.*
- *How to rank events according to their probabilities.*
- *That the least likely events have the least number of boxes in the grid and the most likely events have the most boxes.*
- *That the likelihood of events in a simulation need to be consistent with events in real-world.*

Data Collection

Students collect data to check the accuracy of the simulation. This raises the question of the population being simulated. For example, the data from a school's softball team will be very different from the data from a professional baseball team. After students collect their own data, they can revise the simulation to reflect their data.

Background Information for the Miniature Golf Simulation

The following table summarizes data from 43 players, each playing a complete game of 18 holes on a course in South Carolina. The scores come from teenagers and adults with a wide range of ability levels.

Event	Total Occurrences in 43 Actual Games (18 holes each game)	Average Times an Event Occurred in a Game	Experimental Probability of Events in an Average Game	Theoretical Probability in Simulation
Hole in One	85	1.9	11.0%	16.7% or $^6/_{36}$
2 Strokes	477	11.1	62.0%	22.0% or $^8/_{36}$
3 Strokes	159	3.7	21.0%	25.0% or $^9/_{36}$
4 Strokes	49	1.1	6.0%	16.7% or $^6/_{36}$
5 Strokes	4	.09	.5%	19.0% or $^7/_{36}$

The following table shows one way that the simulation could be revised to make it more realistic. One way to determine the number of boxes for each event is to double the averages. Another way is to multiply the experimental probability by 36.

Event	Average Times an Event Occurred in an Actual Game (18 holes)	Number of Boxes in 36-Box Grid for Simulation
Hole in One	1.9	4
2 Strokes	11.1	22
3 Strokes	3.7	8
4 Strokes	1.1	2
5 Strokes	.09	0

Background Information for the Baseball Simulation

The following data are from the 1994 *Sports Illustrated Sports Almanac* (New York: Little, Brown & Co., 1994), for the Toronto Blue Jays' 1993 season. In 1993, the Blue Jays had a record of 95 wins and 65 losses and were the winners of the World Series. The data are from the 162 games in the regular season. The team had a total of 5,579 at-bats. The team averaged 5.23 runs per game and had a team batting average of .279.

Note: In order to simplify things, strike outs, fly outs, and ground outs have been grouped into the category of outs.

Event	Total Occurrences in 162 Actual Games	Average per Game	Experimental Probability (total/5,579 at-bats)	Theoretical Probability in Simulation
Single	1,038	6.41	.186	.167 or $^6/_{36}$
Double	317	1.96	.057	.055 or $^2/_{36}$
Triple	42	0.26	.008	.083 or $^3/_{36}$
Home run	159	0.98	.028	.111 or $^4/_{36}$
Outs	4,023	24.83	.721	.583 or $^{21}/_{36}$

The table below shows one way to make the simulation more realistic. The number of boxes to assign to each event can be determined by multiplying the experimental probability by 36. An alternative approach is to round the game averages, since they add up to about 34.

Event	Average per Game	Experimental Probability (total/ 5,579 at-bats)	Number of Boxes in 36-Box Grid Simulation
Single	6.41	.186	7
Double	1.96	.057	2
Triple	0.26	.008	0
Home run	0.98	.028	1
Outs	24.83	.721	26

Lesson 11

Simulating a Simple Game

How can you collect and use data to create a simulation of an activity?

In the previous lesson, students tested and revised a simulation. In this lesson, students play a simple tossing game and then create their own simulation to match the results of the game. As they play the game, students gather data to determine the likelihood that different events will occur in the game. They use the data to create a probability line and a game grid. After playing the simulation, students evaluate the realism of the simulation by comparing the simulation results to the results from the tossing game. The process of gathering data and designing a simulation helps prepare students for working independently on their final projects.

Mathematical Goals

- Collect and analyze data to determine the likelihood of real-world events and events in a simulation.
- Use averages to compare sets of data.
- Rank the probabilities of events from never to always (0 to 1).
- Understand that the frequency of events in a simulation should be consistent with the frequency of events represented in the real-world data.
- Create and test a simulation.

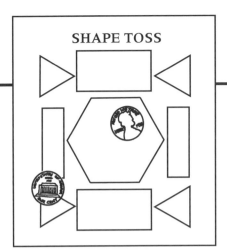

SHAPE TOSS

Materials

Per Group

Reproducible 37, *Shape Toss Game Board*
(optional)

Reproducible 38, *Map Toss Game Board*
(two copies, optional)

5 plastic chips or pennies
(optional)

Pair of number cubes
(two different colors)

Tape and rulers or yardsticks to mark off the
toss lines for the games

Preparation

Select or create a simple game that students can use as the basis
for their simulation. The games described below give students
the opportunity to collect data by doing a physical activity. If
you decide to create your own game, make sure to include at
least four events with a different probability of occurring, so
that students will have a number of outcomes to model and
compare in their simulation.

- Shape Toss: Tape *Shape Toss Game Board* (Reproducible 37) to
  a desk. Players toss a plastic chip or penny onto the board
  from about 12 inches away. Players score points if the penny
  lands inside one of the shapes on the game board. Record the
  frequency of the following events: triangle, 20 points; rectangle, 10 points; hexagon, 5 points; and miss, 0 points.
- Paper Toss: Place a wastebasket against a classroom wall.
  From 3 feet away, players attempt to toss a ball of crumbled
  paper into the basket. Record the frequency of the following
  events: basket, 20 points; near miss (touches the rim), 10

points; wall (misses basket and rim but touches the wall), 5 points; and total miss, 0 points.

- Map Toss: Tape two copies of *Map Toss Game Board* (Reproducible 38) together along the horizontal edge to give players a larger gameboard. Then tape the maps onto the floor. Each player stands 3 feet away from the map and attempts to toss a chip or coin so that it lands inside a country's borders. Students record the frequency of the following events: country, 20 points; border, 10 points; ocean, 5 points; and nowhere (off the board), 0 points. An alternative version is to tape the game board to a desk and have students toss coins from 12 inches away.

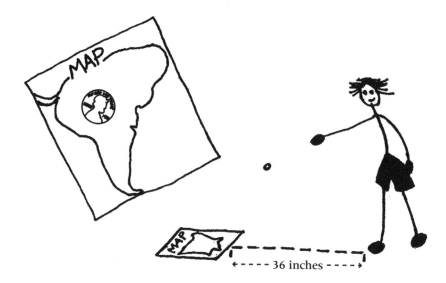

The Map Toss Game

You may want to put tape on the floor to show students where to stand for the tossing games and also create some simple tossing rules. Requiring that students stand straight without bending at the knees or waist will help minimize arguments and ensure some consistency from group to group.

Suggested Lesson Plan

1. Introduction: *Designing a simulation of a tossing game.*

Demonstrate the tossing game that students will simulate. The following memo outlines the steps involved for creating a simulation of the game.

MEMO 3

To: Apprentice Game Designers
From: Directors of New Product
Development

You did a great job testing and revising simulations. Now, we'd like you to design a simulation of one of our tossing games. Here's what you need to do:

- Play the tossing game and record your results.
- Compile the results for the whole class so that you have a lot of data to analyze.
- Use the class data to design a simulation of the tossing game that can be played with two number cubes.
- Test your simulation.

2. Data Collection: *Play the game and record your data.*

Students play the game in small groups, with each player taking at least five turns. Before they begin, have each student make predictions: Which event do they think will happen the most? Which event the least? Why?

Have each group set up a table to record the data that will be used to create the simulation. A table like the one below works well because you can see how many times each of the game's four events occurred:

► **From the Classroom**

My students had an interesting discussion about how many turns they should get. One student argued, "We should do 20. We have to make a simulation, right? It will be more accurate."

► When we played Shape Toss, the pennies bounced off the game boards a lot so "miss" was the most frequent event. Despite this, students had a good time playing and we had enough variety in the outcomes to make the data interesting.

Player	Triangle 20 pts.	Rectangle 10 pts.	Hexagon 5 pts.	Miss 0 pts.	Total Score
Corey	0	2	1	2	25 pts
Delia	1	2	2	1	50 pts
Miguel	2	0	2	2	45 pts
Totals	3	4	5	5	120 pts

3. **Problem Solving:** *Compile the whole-class data and create a probability line.*

Make a graph or table of the results for the whole class. Students determine the average number of times each event occurred and the average scores. Then they determine the experimental probabilities for events in an average game. They use this information to design a simulation that models the class's averages rather than the results of an individual student. In order to keep the design process simple, students will not take into account the distribution of results.

Here's an example for the Shape Toss Game, in which students calculated the averages and the experimental probabilities:

Event	Total Times the Event Happened (for 25 games, 5 tosses each)	Average per Game	Experimental Probability for Events in the Average Game (% of 5 tosses the event happened)
Triangle	10	0.4	8%
Rectangle	25	1.0	20%
Hexagon	40	1.6	32%
Miss	50	2.0	40%
Total	125		100%

Average Score per Game: 26 points

Have students use the experimental probabilities to create a probability line, ranking the events from least likely to most likely. This gives students a visual model for comparing the probabilities of the events and will help students decide how many boxes to assign each event in the game grid. For example:

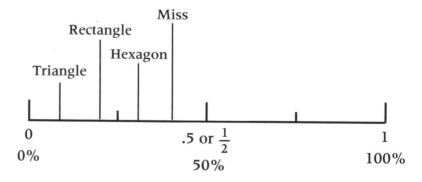

4. Problem Solving: *How can we fill in our game grid so that the simulation will be realistic?*

Draw a 36-box grid to make a number-cube simulation of the tossing game. Discuss how to fill in the grid so that the theoretical probability of events in the simulation will be in proportion to their real-world likelihood. Make sure students are using the class averages to create the grid and not their individual data. In order to test the simulation accurately in the next step, the class needs to agree on how many boxes to give each event.

Here are some sample questions to facilitate making the grid:

- How many boxes should we give to each of the events? why?
- How can we use the percentages from our table to determine the number of boxes that each event should get? (For example, if we know that the coin landed in a rectangle 20% of the time, how many boxes of the grid should we give to the rectangle?)
- Does it matter which boxes on the grid you give to each event? (For example, does it matter if one type of event is in one corner of the grid or spread out?)

Students may find that some events have such low probabilities that they would not get any boxes on a 36-box grid. However, if the events are a part of the actual activity, then students may want to include them in the simulation. (Also, including them will make the simulation more fun to play.) Students may want to give at least one box to the event with the least probability and then adjust the number of boxes for the other events accordingly. An alternative is to use a larger grid, such as a 100-box grid, and use two ten-sided dice or digit cards.

From the Classroom

I filled in the grid so that boxes for each event were next to each other, for example 3 "triangle" events in a row. This way students could visually compare the sizes of the areas for each event. When students created their own grids, they tended to mix up the types of events because they thought it made the games look like more fun.

Sample Game Grid:

Sample Game Grid for Simulation of Shape Toss

Cube #1 (Red) across the top; Cube #2 (Green) down the side

	1	2	3	4	5	6
1	T(20)▲	T(20)▲	T(20)▲	R(10)▮	R(10)▮	R(10)▮
2	R(10)▮	R(10)▮	R(10)▮	R(10)▮	H(5)⬢	H(5)⬢
3	H(5)⬢	H(5)⬢	H(5)⬢	H(5)⬢	H(5)⬢	H(5)⬢
4	H(5)⬢	H(5)⬢	H(5)⬢	H(5)⬢	M(0)	M(0)
5	M(0)	M(0)	M(0)	M(0)	M(0)	M(0)
6	M(0)	M(0)	M(0)	M(0)	M(0)	M(0)

5. Data Collection: *Play the simulation.*

Students play the simulation and record their data, using the same recording method they used when they played the actual game. To facililate comparing the data, students should take the same number of turns as they took in the actual game.

From the Classroom

Some students had the misconception that they would do a lot better when they played the simulation because, unlike the game, the simulation involved no skill. David said, "In the Shape Toss Game it depends on how well you throw the coin. In the simulation, it's just chance."

When Micah played the simulation, she was disappointed that the results didn't match what had happened when she played the actual game. She said, "This doesn't work. We did it all wrong." Tom reminded her to look at the whole-class results for both the simulation and the game.

6. Problem Solving: *Compare results from the simulation and the actual game.*

Compile the class results from the simulation and compare them with the class data from the actual game. A quick way to compare the data is to focus on the average scores from the actual game and the simulation and on one of the events. Since students are familiar with the testing process from the last activity, it is not necessary to compare the results for all the game events.

Compare the class results from the simulation with the class results from the actual game. Write answers to the following questions:

- How does the class's average score from playing the simulation compare with the average from playing the actual game?
- Did the most likely event from the actual game happen the most in the simulation?
- Did the least likely event from the actual game happen the least in the simulation?
- What do you think would happen if you played the simulation 1,000 times?
- Imagine that there is a professional league for Shape Toss players who are very good at getting the coin to land in a shape. Would the simulation you designed be a realistic simulation of the Shape Toss league games? why or why not?

Some students will feel that the simulation is unrealistic because the results don't match their individual results from playing the game. Emphasize to students that the simulation grid is based on the class averages from the game so that it represents the skill level of a typical student as opposed to that of any individual student.

Homework Possibilities

Data Collection

Students collect data on the tossing game from adults or from young children and then revise the simulation grid to match the new set of data.

Writing

Dr. Math letters N–Q (Appendix A).

Lesson 12

Final Project: Design Your Own Simulation

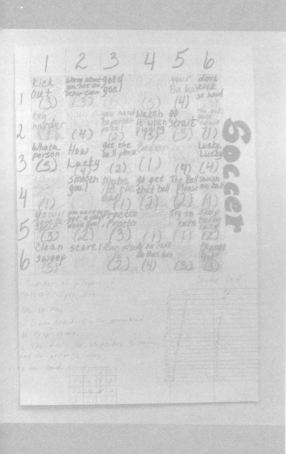

How can you design a simulation of a real-world activity?

In this lesson, students bring together everything they have learned in the unit—along with their own creativity and interests—to produce a final project. Students integrate probability and statistics to design simulations of real-world activities of their own choosing, such as playing a sport or delivering newspapers. After choosing an activity, students identify a range of events that might occur and collect data to determine the probabilities of the events. They use probability lines to rank the likelihood of the events from least likely to most likely. Then they design game grids so that the probability of events in the simulation reflect the real-world probability. Sample student projects are provided in Appendix B.

In Lesson 13, students will share their completed simulations and reflect on what they have learned in the unit.

Mathematical Goals

Apply and extend knowledge of:

- Collecting and representing data.
- Analyzing data to determine probabilities.
- Describing and comparing probabilities.
- Ranking the likelihoods of events on a probability line with a 0–1 scale.
- Modeling the likelihoods of real-world events by creating a simulation.
- Using proportional reasoning to design a simulation in which the frequency of events is consistent with the frequency of events in its real-world counterpart.

Preparation

The following Project Sequence chart suggests a framework for the final project. The timing and sequence of the project may be adjusted to fit the prior experiences of your students. If your students have never undertaken a large project, you may want to build in more opportunities for checking and revising work. On the other hand, if your students are used to large assignments such as this one, you may want to let them determine the structure and sequence. In either case, a good way to help keep students on track is to pair them up with partners who serve as "simulation consultants." Although each student works on his or her project individually, the consultants provide feedback on the simulation and check to make sure all the steps are being followed.

Since the final project is an assessment, it is essential that students understand from the start how their work will be evaluated. You may want to use the sample quality criteria (in Step 3) or involve students in developing a new version.

The suggested sequence for working on the project is divided into three parts: getting started, independent work, and sharing the projects. Each part is described in greater detail in the suggested lesson plans for Lessons 12 and 13. The first and last parts will take about two class periods each. The amount of time needed for independent work will vary depending on whether students will work on the project outside of class or in class. In the former case, allow about one-and-a-half to two weeks for students to complete the project. In the meantime, you can begin another unit or other math work in class. If students will work on the project during class time, allow from three to five class periods.

Project Sequence Chart

	Steps	Materials Needed Per Student	Per Class
Lesson 12 **2 class periods**	*Getting Started* Give and clarify the assignment Students brainstorm possibilities for simulations Students describe their ideas and how they will collect data Establish quality criteria for assessing the projects	Reproducible 39, *Final Project: Design a Simulation* Reproducible 40, *Project Planning Sheet*	Reproducible 31, *Miniature Golf Simulation* (optional transparency) Reproducible 33, *Simulation Baseball* (optional transparency)
Lesson 12 **3+ class periods***	*Independent Work* Independent work on the project at home or in class Set due dates as needed for check points and revisions	Reproducible 41, *Final Project Cover Sheet*	
Lesson 13 **1–2 class periods**	*Sharing the Projects* Students present their simulations Students play one another's games Students reflect on their experiences working on the projects	Reproducible 42, *Simulation Testing Sheet*	

*Amount of time for independent work will vary depending on whether work will be done in class or outside of class.

Suggested Lesson Plan

1. Introduction: *Assign and discuss the final project.*

Final Project: Design a Simulation (Reproducible 39) describes the steps of the assignment, beginning with the selection of an activity to simulate. Ask students to brainstorm and share ideas for their simulations. Students should choose topics they know well so that they can use their knowledge to help make the simulations more realistic.

Reproducible 39

2. Writing: *Choose a topic and plan your research.*

The *Project Planning Sheet* (Reproducible 40) provides questions to help students choose an activity to simulate, identify events in the activity, and plan how they will collect data. You may want to use the grids for the two simulations from Lesson 10 (Reproducibles 31 and 33) to help generate ideas about what different kinds of simulations might look like.

Emphasize the importance of collecting a lot of data. For example, the scores from one bowling game would not provide enough data to make a realistic simulation.

Reviewing the project planning sheets will help you identify students that may need some assistance. The following table shows a range of student work along with comments on the strengths or weaknesses of the work:

Student Work and Comments

Step 1. Describe Topic

I am planning to simulate basketball. I play basketball every day. I am sure a majority of the students here are interested in basketball that's why I chose it.

Student has a lot of experience with the chosen topic. Projects tend to turn out better when students are familiar with the topic.

Step 2. List of Events (for basketball)

Defensive foul, traveling, lay-up, make shot, miss shot, offensive foul, backcourt violation, ball goes out of bounds, ball stolen, blocked shot, miss shot, get rebound.

Having so many events can lead to a very complicated simulation. Suggest cutting events or combining some under a more general heading. For example, "offensive foul" and "backcourt violation" could be combined into "turnover."

Step 2. List of events (for house building)
Pour foundation, have it inspected, build frame, make blueprints, and buy supplies.

All the events on this list have the same likelihood of occurring—they are all essential steps in the house-building process. Suggest revising the list to include events that have different likelihoods of occurring, such as "window breaks."

Step 3. Data Collection Plan

I would interview my family and friends. Find out how many people have dogs in the 7th grade and interview them. Keep a record of what happens when I walk my dog.

Student plans to collect data from interviews as well as from her own experience.

Step 3. Data collection plan.
I already know tons about the topic.

This student does not have a plan for collecting data. Suggest ways of collecting data on topic. If topic is difficult to research, student may want to select another topic.

3. Discussion: *Establish quality criteria.*

After students have chosen an activity and started collecting data, they will understand the assignment well enough to think about how to assess the projects. Involving students in deciding the assessment criteria for their projects gives them a sense of ownership and clarifies expectations.

The sample quality criteria may be used as is, or as a starting point for students to develop their own criteria.

ASSESSMENT CRITERIA

Well Done

- Appropriate real-world data were collected and analyzed.

- The order of the events on the probability line is consistent with the real-world data.

- The chances of getting events in the simulation are consistent with the order of the events in the probability line. (For example, the least likely event has the least number of boxes on the game grid and the most likely event has the most boxes in the game grid.)

- Probabilities of events in the simulation are accurately described as fractions, decimals, percents, or ratios.

- The report is clearly written and informative.

- Game board is color-coded so that each type of event has a different color.

Acceptable

- Meets at least the first four conditions listed for Well Done.

Unacceptable

- No data collected.

- Pieces of project are missing.

- No apparent connection between game grid, probability line, and real-world activity.

Some students figured out the probabilities
of different events by gathering lots
of quantitative data, figuring out the
percentages, and dividing the grid accordingly.
Others made more qualitative judgments
about things that were "most likely" or "least
likely" to happen. One student described
how he collected data for a surfboarding
simulation: "I went to a boat show. I talked to
a guy and he told me about events that
someone would likely be able to do."

4. Data Collection: *What's the probability of each event in the simulation?*

Students begin their independent work on the project by figuring out how to collect data. The type of data and the way the data are collected will vary depending on the activities students have chosen to simulate. For some topics, such as baseball, there is a lot of quantitative data available in reference books or school team records. Students can also gather their own data by watching or doing the activity themselves and keeping a tally of different events or by interviewing people who know a lot about the topic to determine the likelihood of events.

> • I am planning to simulate a basketball game called "courtesy".
> • I play this game often with my brother at home.
>
> To collect data, I will have 7 people take 8 shots from each zone. (zones drawn on back) I will record how many are made or missed in each zone.

> I took my data from my own experiences in playing the flute, my friends who play flute, and my flute teacher. Which each person I talked to, we discussed the chances of several different things that can happen while playing the flute.

> I chose nine all-time great players, one at each position plus a designated hitter from the National League and the American League. I looked up in the Baseball Encyclopedia (9th Edition, MacMillan Publishing Company) the following lifetime statistics on each player: at bats, walks, hits, home runs, triples, doubles, and strikeouts. I entered these on a spreadsheet in Microsoft Works.

> My topic is weather, which I chose because I experience it every day. It controls what we wear and do. I designed my simulation to be more realistic by collecting data by watching predictions on television, looking in almanacs from past years, calling the weather on the telephone, using the forecast in the newspaper for almost every day in April, reading books and encyclopedias, my own and other people's experiences, and common sense.

5. Problem Solving: *Create the probability line and the simulation grid.*

After students collect and analyze their data, they use the data to create a probability line. The completed probability line will help students figure out how to fill in their simulation grid. Students may want to use 36-box grids and two number cubes like the simulations in the previous lessons. Alternatively, students can choose to use game pieces, such as two spinners or ten-sided dice, and draw grids to reflect all the possible outcomes. Some students may also create simulations with multiple grids, each showing the probabilities for a particular player or team.

As students work on the rest of the project, you may want to schedule checkpoints and feedback sessions to help keep them on track. For example, by reviewing rough drafts of several parts of the project you can identify areas in which individual students are having problems. In addition, students might try out one another's simulations as they are being developed. Make sure to allow students enough time to think about feedback and revise their simulations.

6. Writing: *Prepare the projects.*

Final Project Cover Sheet (Reproducible 41) provides a format to help students summarize essential information about their simulations and how they designed them. This information will help you assess the projects in the next lesson. In point 4 on the cover sheet, students use a table to summarize the probabilities for each event. For example, a table for the Miniature Golf simulation from Lesson 10 would like this:

Events	Number of Boxes You Gave the Event in Your Simulation Grid	Probability of Event (as a percentage, ratio, fraction, or decimal)
Hole in One	6	$^6/_{36}$ or .167
2 Strokes	8	$^8/_{36}$ or .222
3 Strokes	9	$^9/_{36}$ or .25
4 Strokes	6	$^6/_{36}$ or .167
5 Strokes	7	$^7/_{37}$ or .194

▶ **From the Classroom**

Students tried out their rough drafts of the simulations with a partner. Playing the games gave students a good sense of what improvements they might want to make. Some students wanted to revamp their grids based on their scores from playing one time. I pointed out that they hadn't gathered enough data to do an accurate test. We discussed what students would do if they wanted to test the realism of the simulations.

Reproducible 41

▶ **From the Classroom**

I gave out manila folders for students to use to design the final versions of the simulations. Students drew the grid game boards and the probability lines on the folders and kept their reports and rules inside them. The folder helped contain the size of the game boards and made it easy to store the simulations.

▶ *I had groups of students share rough drafts of their simulations. Some problems students found were (1) a mismatch between the probability scale and the grid, where the more frequent events showed up infrequently on the grid; (2) too many events in the simulation, which made it confusing; (3) events that had extremely high and unrealistic probabilities of occurring.*

I found that once students could put 5–10 events in order, the grid was easier to create. I knew the time we devoted to the rough drafts was worthwhile when I saw the dramatic improvements in the final versions.

Lesson 13

Project Seminar: Testing the Simulation Games

What kinds of simulations have you and your classmates designed? How did you make your simulations realistic?

In this lesson, students present their projects to their classmates and test one another's simulations. Playing their classmates' simulations helps students appreciate different approaches to the project and encourages them to think about how well their own work meets the quality criteria. After writing feedback on their partners' games, students reflect on what they've learned in the unit.

Mathematical Goals

- Describe and compare the probabilities of real-world situations and simulations.
- Share methods for collecting and analyzing data and for modeling situations.
- Appreciate the value and variety of mathematics used in completing the final project.

Materials

Per Student

Reproducible 41, *Final Project Cover Sheet* (from Lesson 12)

Reproducible 42, *Simulation Testing Sheet*

Suggested Lesson Plan

1. Sharing: *Present the simulation games.*

Students present their simulations to their classmates. Here are two ways to organize the class presentations:

- Whole-class presentations: Students give brief descriptions of their simulations and how they designed them.
- Small-group presentation: In groups of two, three, or four, students take turns being "interviewers" and "presenters." The interviewers ask the presenters questions like those on *Final Project Cover Sheet* (Reproducible 41).

Reproducible 41

▶ **From the Classroom**

I had students present their projects to the whole class because I wanted to highlight the importance of the project and the work students had done. I gave out a list of questions for students to use as a guideline for their presentations. After all the students had presented, I asked each student to find partners to test their simulation. Students really liked having an opportunity to play each other's simulations.

▶ *Many students were uncomfortable about speaking in front of the whole class, so I made the presentations voluntary. Still, I did want each student to show and explain their simulation to some of their classmates. I asked students to get into groups of two and had them describe their project and then test their partner's simulation. We spent two class periods sharing and testing the simulations.*

Reproducible 42

2. Sharing: *Testing the simulations.*

Students can trade and test the simulations in small groups, or you can set up a kind of simulation fair in which students walk around the classroom and choose simulations they'd like to test.

The questions on *Simulation Testing Sheet* (Reproducible 42) guide students on providing constructive feedback on their classmate's simulations. Have students fill out the sheets right after they test a simulation.

▶ From the Classroom

I was surprised that Matthew was so excited to have other students play his simulation. When we started the projects he seemed very frustrated because he couldn't think of an idea for his simulation. He eventually decided to do a simulation of professional tennis, a sport with which he is very familiar. He designed an outcome grid that lets the server win when he or she rolls an even number or a three. Matthew explained, "The server usually wins, so there's a slightly better chance of winning if you are the server." As he discussed the simulation with his classmates, he was clearly proud of all the work he had put into the project.

Tess was upset because when she played her basketball simulation with her classmates the scores were much different from what she had expected. She had carefully collected data and set up her grid, but the experimental results were way off. She thought that she had done something wrong and she was ready to revise it. I reminded her what we had learned about the law of large numbers at the beginning of the unit: If she played the simulation many times, the results would be closer to the theoretical probablities.

3. Discussion: *How did you design your simulation?*

Students discuss their experiences working on the project and talk about what they have learned. Some sample questions include:

- What did you find out when other students tested your simulation?
- How many times would you recommend playing a simulation to see if it is realistic?
- How would you change your simulation to make it more realistic?
- How would you change your simulation to make it more fun to play?

▶ **From the Classroom**

Students discussed the trade-off between making a simulation realistic and making it a fun game to play. Pat designed a simulation of volleyball that was quite realistic but was boring to play because it took a while to score a point. Some students suggested having unlikely events occur more often than they would in real life to make the games more exciting.

4. Assessment: *Use the quality criteria to evaluate the projects.*

The students' completed final project cover sheets are helpful for evaluating student work on some key components of the project. The information on the sheet makes it easy to compare the likelihood of the real-world events with the probability in the simulations. Sample student projects are provided in Appendix B.

5. Student Self-Assessment: *Reflecting on the project.*

TO THE STUDENT

1. What do you like best about your simulation game?
   - What would you do differently if you design another simulation?
   - What tips would you give to other students who wanted to make a realistic simulation game?
   - What does your project show about what you learned during the unit? What are some things you learned that your project doesn't show?

Appendix A

"Dear Dr. Math"

This appendix is a collection of "advice column" letters containing questions about probability. In answering these letters, students take on the role of math experts. They can be as creative as they like in answering the letters—as long as they respond to the letter writer's question.

You can use these letters in a variety of ways: as assessments; as homework; as opportunities for students to reflect on and synthesize content in the unit; and as catalysts for small-group or whole-class discussions. To assist you in evaluating students' work, a list of key points for each letter is provided at the end of the section.

"Dear Dr. Math" Letters

A. Dear Dr. Math,

I just don't get it! My friend and I each flipped a coin 10 times. My friend got 8 heads and I only got 2 heads. We thought that we each had a 50% chance of getting heads, but neither of us got 5 heads! Why did this happen? Should we practice flipping coins?

Sooooo Confused

Letter(s)	When to Use
A–D	Any time after Lesson 2
E	Any time after Lesson 3
F–H	Any time after Lesson 4
I	Any time after Lesson 5
J, K	Any time after Lesson 8
L, M	Any time after Lesson 9
N–P	Any time after Lesson 11
Q	Any time in the unit after students have worked on a few Dr. Math letters

B. Dear Dr. Math,

My best friend and I are going to the town carnival. Every year they have a booth called the Five Alive booth where if you roll a number cube and get a 5 you win. I told my friend that I was definitely going to win a lot at the Five Alive booth because 5 is my lucky number. My friend said that all of the numbers on the cube have the same chance so 5 can't be luckier for me than any other number. What do you think?

Luke Key

C. Dear Dr. Math,

I am the new Carnival Inspector. My job is to check all carnival booths to make sure that players get at least a 50% chance of winning at each booth. I was planning to take 10 turns at each booth as my test, but my boss suggested that I take 100 turns at each booth. I don't understand what the difference is. Can't I just take 10 turns and multiply the results by 10 to find out what I would get if I took 100 turns?

Carnival Inspector Brown

D. Dear Dr. Math,

I just got a new job as a game tester for the AllPlay Company. My first assignment is to test a game in which players toss objects with different shapes. There are three objects and all of them are strange because they are not symmetrical. One looks like a bottle cap, one looks like a little cup, and one looks like a kid's crayon with one side flat and one side round. For each object, I have to figure out the chances of it landing on each side. What should I do?

New AllPlay Employee

E. Dear Dr. Math,

My two best friends keep arguing about basketball. Sara says the probability of making a free throw is always 50%. Either you get it in or you miss, so it's 50–50. Andrea says she makes 70% of her free throws, so the probability can't always be 50%. Who is right and how can I convince them so they stop arguing?

Beebee Hoop

F. Dear Dr. Math,

In five spins of this spinner (see my drawing), Sophie got 4 greens and 1 red. Marcus also had five turns and got 1 green and 4 reds. I think Marcus is more likely to get green on the next turn, since he got fewer greens so far. My friend thinks it's impossible to predict what Sophie and Marcus will spin. Who do you think is correct?

Spin Rrrr

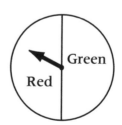

G. Dear Dr. Math,

I can't seem to win at the Cover-Up Game. When I make my game card, I put the colors or words that I think will come up the most in the boxes near the center of the card. I put the ones that won't come up much in the corners. This strategy for making a game card doesn't seem to work well. Can you suggest a better one?

Wants T. Winn

H. Dear Dr. Math,

My friend and I have been arguing about the Cover-Up Game. She says she can make a new spinner and a game card with 12 boxes so that she will always cover the card in exactly 12 spins. That doesn't seem possible to me, but she insists she can. Do you think it is possible? How can she do it?

Ida N. Know

I. Dear Dr. Math,

My community center is having a carnival next weekend. I'm running one of the game booths. I'm going to call it Playing the Blues because you will win if you spin a spinner and land on blue. My assistant has designed three different spinners we could use (see drawings). I want the one that will allow me to give out the least number of prizes. Which is the best spinner for me to use? The second best spinner? How did you figure it out?

Less P. Rizes

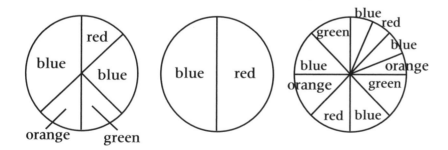

J. Dear Dr. Math,

One afternoon, my friend and I designed a new game for two players, called KimJo. The rules are:

Roll two number cubes.

Subtract the smaller number from the larger number.

Player A gets a point if the difference is 1, 3, or 5.

Player B gets a point if the difference is 0, 2, or 4.

The player with the most points after 9 turns wins.

Then our friend, Tom, came over and wanted to play. We couldn't figure out how to change the rules so that it would be fair for three players. Help! What should we do?

Kimberly and Joseph

K. Dear Dr. Math,

I designed a number-cube game called Double or Nothing for my carnival booth. Players roll two number cubes and they win a prize if they get doubles. I need to figure out how many prizes to buy. I expect that the game will be played about 200 times. About how many prizes do you think I will give out? Tell me how you figured it out so I'll be able to do it myself the next time.

Booth Owner

L. Dear Dr. Math,

The Federal Games Association (FGA) has really gotten tough! Before I can sell my new game in stores, the label has to show the chances of winning in at least three different ways.

In my game, you roll two number cubes and multiply the numbers that come up. You win if the product is even. I know an even product happens in 27 out of the 36 possible combinations. But how can I show the chances of winning my game in three different ways?

President, Fun Factory Games Guild

M. Dear Dr. Math,

I am very upset! My school had a raffle. They sold 1,000 tickets and they were raffling off 10 really cool prizes. I bought 5 tickets and my friend Joe bought 1 ticket. Yesterday they drew the tickets out of a hat. Joe won a prize. I was so excited because I figured I would win 5 prizes since I had bought five times as many tickets as Joe. But I didn't win 5 prizes; in fact, I didn't win anything! What happened? Why did Joe win with 1 ticket and I didn't win but had 5 tickets?

Five Tickets, No Prizes

N. Dear Dr. Math,

Maria and Carla both play on my basketball team at school. Last week we had a game and the other team made a technical foul. Our coach had to choose one of our five players on the court at the time of the foul to take the shot. I thought he would pick Maria because she has made 100% of her foul shots this season. But the coach picked Carla who has made only 60% of her shots this season. I thought 100% was better than 60%. Here are their statistics for the season:

Maria   2 shots attempted   2 shots made

Carla   100 shots attempted   60 shots made

Can you please explain this to me?

Team Manager and Record Keeper

O. Dear Dr. Math,

My friend and I want to make a simulation game of softball. We want the scores in the simulation to be like the scores real middle school students get. How can we collect the data we need? How much data should we collect?

Hi Score

P. Dear Dr. Math,

I made a simulation game of basketball free throws, using number cubes. To start, I collected a lot of data. Four of my friends shot 25 free throws each, while I recorded the number of baskets, near misses (hit the rim), and total misses (airballs).

Here are my data:

baskets made   60 out of 100 = 60%

near misses   25 out of 100 = 25%

total misses   15 out of 100 = 15%

I'm having trouble filling in the 36-box game grid. I put "total miss" in 15 of the boxes since it was 15%. Now I don't have enough boxes left for baskets made or near misses. What should I do?

Freda Throe

Q. Dear AllPlay Game Designers,

I'm so bored! I love to answer students' questions about probability, but I haven't received any letters in over a month!! Is there something about probability that's been confusing you lately? Have you designed a new game you'd like me to test? Can you make up a probability problem for me to solve? Please write to me!

Desperate Dr. Math

Key Points for Assessing Students' Responses

The list below provides some key points that students may include in their responses to the "Dear Dr. Math" letters. You can use this list to evaluate students' understanding of the mathematics content.

Letter A

- When the number of trials is small, outcomes vary widely. If two people do the same experiment with 10 trials, it is likely that they will not get the same results.

- As the number of trials increases, the experimental probability approaches the theoretical probability. Ten trials is not sufficient to expect the outcome to always reflect the theoretical probabilities.

- Practice in flipping coins does not affect the chances that a coin will land on heads.

Letter B

- All six numbers on a number cube have the same probability of being tossed.
- An individual's "luck" does not affect the probabilities of the different outcomes.

Letter C

- The more trials conducted, the closer the experimental probability will get to the theoretical probability and the better the indication of the chances at the booth.
- In a small number of trials you can get unexpected results, which makes it a less fair test.

Letter D

- When probabilities cannot be determined theoretically, they can be determined experimentally.
- Many trials are needed in an experiment in order to get an accurate picture of the probabilities.

Letter E

- Having two possible outcomes does not imply that those outcomes are equally likely.
- Gathering data on free-throw scores can help you figure out the probability of getting a free throw.

Letter F

- Events like successive spins of a spinner and coin tosses are independent. This means that the probability of getting a color on a given spin is not affected by what happened on prior spins. The spinner doesn't remember what happened on the previous spins.
- It is equally likely for the arrow to land on the red or green parts because they each take up half the area of the spinner.

Letter G

The number of boxes on the game card that you assign to each outcome is what matters, not the location of the boxes. The colors or words that have the highest probability of being spun should have the most boxes on the game card and those with the lowest probability should have the fewest.

Letter H

If there is only one possible outcome, its probability is 1 or 100%. The solution to the problem is a spinner with only one outcome and a game card with that outcome in each box.

Letter I

- If a color takes up a larger area of the circle, it is likely to be spun proportionally more frequently than a color that takes up a smaller portion.
- The probability of getting a color depends on its area in the circle and not the number of parts that have that color.
- The chances of getting blue in each of the spinners can be described by using fractions, percents, or decimals (spinner A—$\frac{5}{8}$, spinner B—$\frac{1}{2}$, spinner C—$\frac{6}{16}$).

Letter J

By making an outcome grid, you can figure out the probability of getting each of the differences. Then you can assign the differences to the three players so that each player has a $\frac{12}{36}$ probability of winning. For example, player A scores for a difference of 0 or 3; B for 1 or 5; and C for 4 or 8.

Letter K

- There are 36 possible outcomes when you toss two number cubes. The probability of getting doubles is 6 out of 36 or $\frac{1}{6}$.
- Multiply 200 by the probability (.167) to estimate the number of doubles (33.4) that will occur. The number of doubles is likely to be close to 33, but not necessarily exactly 33.

Letter L

- Figure out the chances of winning the game—$\frac{3}{4}$.
- Use at least three of the following ways to describe the chances of winning: percent, fraction, ratio, decimal.

Letter M

- The probability of winning a prize for someone who buys one ticket is the ratio of the number of prizes divided by the total number of tickets sold ($\frac{10}{1000}$ or $\frac{1}{100}$). This probability goes up to only $\frac{5}{100}$ for someone who buys five tickets.
- Having five times as many tickets doesn't mean that a person will win five times as many prizes.

Letter N

There is a lot more data on Carla's performance, which makes it a better indicator of how she will perform than Maria's data. The law of large numbers brings out the importance of basing decisions on a lot of data.

Letter O

- Data needs to be collected from the actual event. Since the simulation is about middle school teams, the data must come from middle school games.
- Data from many games would give a more accurate picture of the probabilities than data from a few games.

Letter P

- The probabilities in the simulation need to reflect the probabilities in the actual sport.
- A 15% probability in the actual sport should be entered into 15% of the boxes in the grid, not 15 boxes.

Letter Q

This problem gives students the opportunity to articulate problems or questions they have about probability. It has to be used as an informal assessment, to get a sense of what students are having difficulty with. Alternatively, students can write questions about concepts they understand and then write the responses.

Sample Student Projects

Simulation of Playing Piano

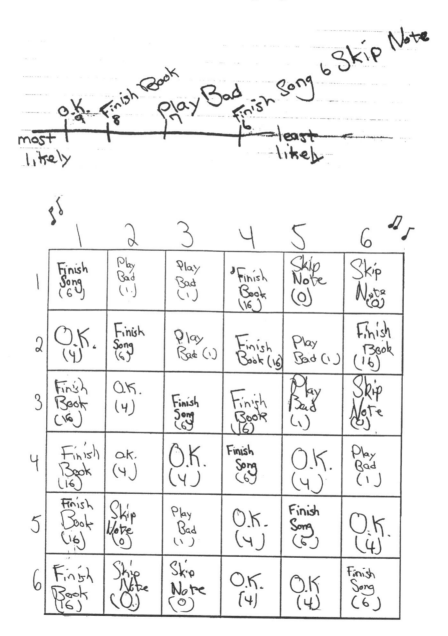

I designed my simulation by really thinking hard and with ideas that my piano teacher gave me.

Basketball Example

Black / Red	1	2	3	4	5	6
1	OUT OF BOUNDS (0)	DUNK (2)	ALLEY-OOP (2)	BRICK (0)	STEAL (Lose turn)	3-POINTER (3)
2	ALLEY-OOP (2)	LAYUP (2)	SWISH (2)	FOUL SHOT (1)	3-POINTER (3)	hookshot (2)
3	BRICK (0)	STEAL (Lose turn)	DUNK (2)	LAYUP (2)	AIRBALL (0)	NICE SHOT! (2)
4	NICE SHOT! (2)	FOUL SHOT (1)	hookshot (2)	SWISH (2)	FOUL SHOT (1)	LAYUP (2)
5	hookshot (2)	3-POINTER (3)	BRICK (0)	STEAL (lose turn)	hookshot (2)	NICE SHOT! (2)
6	NICE SHOT! (2)	SWISH (2)	AIRBALL (0)	3-POINTER (3)	DUNK (2)	OUT OF BOUNDS (0)

Bowling Example

Rough Draft

(C) LIKELIHOODS   (B) SOURCES OF DATA

(C)   This bowling game is from the point of view that you are a professional bowler. Most professional bowlers average a 120. The odds are about the same in this game as in the real games on t.v. In this game you have about one-twelveth a chance of getting a strike, one-fifth a chance of getting a spare, one-third of getting a 10, one-fourth of getting a 9, one-nineth of getting an 8, and one-thirtysixth of getting a 7. Those are the odds of the bowlers on the television. With this game the average is 129. To get this average I added up all points on grid, divided that number by 36, and then times it by 10.

(b)   My major sources were my father, the World Book Encyclopedia, and watching bowling on t.v.

(D) RULES

(1) First role the two dice (red + black)

(2) Look on chart, grid to see how many points you get.

(3) You get the amount of points that is in the middle of the square in parentheses.

(4) After each player roles the two dice 10 times the game is over.

(5) Add up all your points for each player

(6) Player with the most points wins

not likely |⑦ (STRIKE) ⑧ (SPARE) ⑨ ⑩| most likely

CANDLEPIN
PROFESSIONAL BOWLING

RED BLACK	1	2	3	4	5	6
1	STRIKE (20)	(8)	(10)	(9)	(10)	(7)
2	(10)	SPARE (15)	(9)	SPARE (15)	(10)	SPARE (15)
3	(8)	(9)	STRIKE (20)	(9)	(8)	(10)
4	(10)	(9)	(9)	SPARE (15)	(10)	(10)
5	(8)	(10)	(9)	(10)	SPARE (15)	(10)
6	(10)	(9)	(10)	SPARE (15)	(9)	SPARE (15)

40 STRIKE - ²/18
105 SPARE - ⁷/5

130 10 - ¹³/3
81 9 - ⁹/4
32 8 - ⁴/9
7 7 - ¹/36

36)485
108
19

15/36) 465.0
36
186
72
330
324
= 12.9

Skating Example

Report on My Math Simulation Game

I did a simulation game of the Women's Olympic Figure Skating Event. I chose this topic because I know that many girls such as myself have always dreamed of competing in this particular Olympic event, and with my simulation game that dream is made possible. I also chose it because I love figure skating, and I wanted to find out more about the scores that people get.

The data that I collected during my research was mainly from a video tape that I have of the Technical and Free programs in the 1994 Women's Olympic Figure Skating Event. Some of my background information however came from old issues of The Boston Globe in the library. From my research I found out that 5.7, 5.8, and 5.6 are the three scores that occur most in this event.

I designed my game grid according to the probability of each score occurring during the Women's Olympic Figure Skating Event according to my research. I also color coded each number to make it more pleasing to the eye.

When I tested my game with my family they didn't have any trouble understanding the rules, and they seemed to enjoy it quite a bit. My sister Leanna especially enjoyed it because she won with a score of 117.3.

I thoroughly enjoyed designing this simulation, because I got to learn a lot about probabilities, percents, and ratios. Those three things were what I based all of my decisions on for this project, and I can continue to use that way of thinking for my every day life.

Yellow / Green	1	2	3	4	5	6
1	5.7	5.9	5.4	5.8	5.5	5.9
2	5.4	4.9	5.7	5.3	5.0	5.8
3	5.8	5.2	5.6	4.7	4.6	5.6
4	4.3	4.2	4.0	5.5	5.7	4.5
5	5.2	5.6	5.9	5.3	5.6	5.1
6	5.8	4.4	5.7	5.8	5.5	5.7

1994

Dear Family,

Our class will soon be starting a new mathematics unit called *Chance Encounters: Probability in Games and Simulations*. The unit focuses on key topics in probability and statistics that have been recommended for middle-school students by the National Council of Teachers of Mathematics. It also provides opportunities for students to apply and extend their knowledge of percents, fractions, decimals, and ratios.

Throughout the unit, students will use mathematics to analyze games and simulations. They will explore ways of improving games and simulations and they will create their own. In addition, students will investigate the role of probability in different real-world situations, such as sports events. Here are some of the questions students will investigate:

- How can we compare the probabilities of different events?
- How can we determine whether or not a game is fair?
- How can we determine the probability of winning a game?
- How can we describe probabilities in different ways, such as with fractions, percentages, graphs, and diagrams?
- How can we design a game that simulates the probabilities of different events, such as hitting a home run or striking out while playing baseball?

You can help your child by playing and discussing some of the games in the unit or some old family favorites. Which games are based on chance? Which games give players better chances of winning? Encourage your child to share with you the games and simulations he or she is creating, and talk about the ways in which probability is used in everyday life.

Sincerely,

Carnival Games

Ticket

A. Get Ahead Booth

Toss a coin.

Heads = 1 Ticket
Tails = 0

B. Lucky 3s Booth

Roll a number cube.

3 = 1 Ticket
1, 2, 4, 5, or 6 = 0

C. Evens or Odds Booth

Roll a number cube.

2, 4, or 6 = 1 Ticket
1, 3, or 5 = 0

D. Pick a Number Booth

Predict what number you will roll. Then, roll a number cube.

Prediction is True = 1 Ticket
If not = 0

E. Coin and Cube Booth

Toss a coin and roll a number cube.

Tails & 3, 4, 5, or 6 = 1 Ticket
Anything else = 0

F. Teens Only Booth

Roll a number cube 2 times. Make a 2-digit number.
(You can reverse the order of the digits.)

13, 14, 15, or 16 = 1 Ticket
Anything else = 0

Rules: Players take turns. On your turn, pick the booth you want to play and try to win a ticket. During a game, you can go to all the booths, some of them, or just one. See how many tickets you can win in 10 turns.

Chance Encounters

Name(s) —————

3 6 Carnival Games Scoresheet

Player One

Turn	Booth(Letter)	Tickets
1		
2		
3		
4		
5		
6		
7		
8		
9		
10		
Total Number of Tickets		
Number of Turns with 0 Tickets		

Player Two

Turn	Booth(Letter)	Tickets
1		
2		
3		
4		
5		
6		
7		
8		
9		
10		
Total Number of Tickets		
Number of Turns with 0 Tickets		

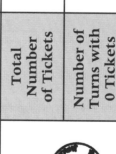

Which booths did you go to? Why?
What would you do differently if you played again?

Chance Encounters

Reproducible 3

Improving the Carnival Games

1. Rate the Carnival Games on a scale of 1-5. Explain why you picked this rating.

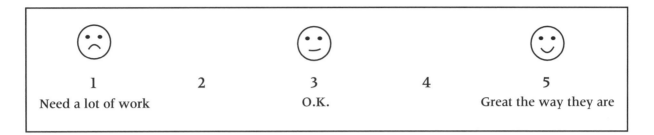

2. Brainstorm ways of changing the games.

   a. How could you change a booth or design a new one to make it *more likely* for players to win tickets?

   b. How could you change a booth or design a new one to make it *less likely* for players to win tickets?

3. Design at least one new booth.

Strip Graph Templates

Chance Encounters

What Might Happen in 20 Turns at One of the Carnival Booths?

1. Make predictions.

- How many wins do you think you will get in 20 turns? ☐

- What do you think the highest number of wins in the class will be? ☐

    The lowest? ☐

- What do you think the most common number of wins will be? ☐

2. Conduct the experiment and record your results.

With a partner, take turns tossing a coin or number cube. Record the results on a strip graph, like the ones below. Before each toss, predict what you will get. When you are done, color in the boxes where you would win tickets.

Sample Strip Graphs:

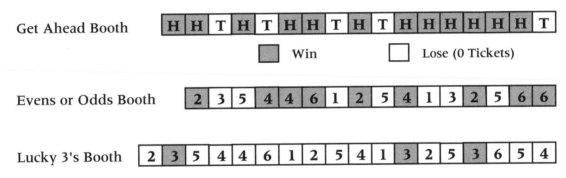

Get Ahead Booth | H | H | T | H | T | H | H | T | H | T | H | H | H | H | H | T |

☐ Win   ☐ Lose (0 Tickets)

Evens or Odds Booth | 2 | 3 | 5 | 4 | 4 | 6 | 1 | 2 | 5 | 4 | 1 | 3 | 2 | 5 | 6 | 6 |

Lucky 3's Booth | 2 | 3 | 5 | 4 | 4 | 6 | 1 | 2 | 5 | 4 | 1 | 3 | 2 | 5 | 3 | 6 | 5 | 4 |

	Your Results	Class Results
Total number of wins		
Longest number of wins in a row		
Highest number of wins in class		
Lowest number of wins in class		
Most common number of wins(mode)		

Unfinished Report

Adrianna and Erik did an experiment with a number cube, but they didn't finish writing their report. Here's what they wrote:

We tossed a number cube 40 times to find out how many odd and even numbers we would get. The number cube has the numbers 1,2,3,4,5,and 6 on it.

We predicted that we would get about 20 odd numbers and 20 even ones.

When we tossed the cube, we wrote down an O if we got an odd number and an E if we got an even one.

O	O	E	E	O	O	O	O	O	O
O	O	E	E	O	O	E	E	E	O
O	E	E	O	O	O	O	E	O	E
O	E	E	O	E	E	O	E	O	O

Finish writing the report.

1. Make a table, frequency graph, or bar graph of the results on a separate sheet of paper.

2. What fraction or percent of the 40 tosses were odd numbers? even numbers? (That's called the *experimental probability*.)

   Experimental probability of getting an odd number: _____

   Experimental probability of getting an even number: _____

3. What do you think the results would be if Adrianna and Erik had tossed the number cube 1,000 times? Why?

4. How many tosses do you think it would take to get about **80 even numbers**? Why?

How Likely Is It?

1. How likely are different events on a typical school day?

   Here are some events that might happen during a day at school. Order these events from *least likely* to happen to *most likely* to happen by putting them on a probability line.

   A. Get to school on time.   B. Have a fire drill.

   C. Get assigned homework.   D. Eat a sandwich for lunch.

   E. Someone in your class is absent.   F. See a famous movie star.

   G. See someone wearing sneakers.   H. Go to the gym.

   I. Add your own event:_____.

   J. Add your own event:_____.

Probability Line

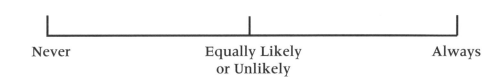

```
       Never           Equally Likely          Always
                         or Unlikely
```

2. For each of the following, list at least *two* real-world events that will:

   a. **definitely** happen tomorrow   b. **probably** happen tomorrow

   c. **probably not** happen tomorrow   d. **never** happen tomorrow

Hoping for Snow

The advertisement below is an actual ad from a Massachusetts newspaper. Read it and answer the following questions.

©1993 Carol L. Bartolomucci

1. Do you think that this is a good deal? Why or why not?

2. If this advertisement appeared in your area, how could you get information to figure out your chances of getting a refund? What kind of information would you want?

3. What do you think your chances of getting a refund would be?

4. Where in the United States would you have better chances of getting a refund? worse chances?

5. Design your own advertisement that involves chance.

The Cover-Up Game

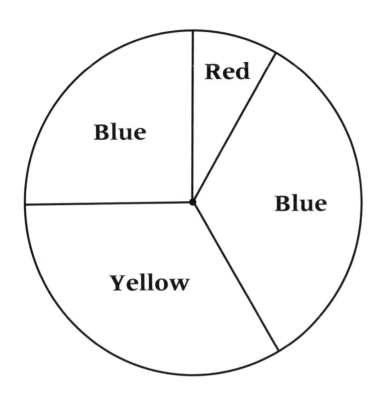

How to Play the Game:
When you spin a color, put an X on one box with that color on your game card. If you do not need that color, it is scored as an Extra. Put a tally mark in the Extras table.

The game ends when you put X's over all the boxes on your game card.

The goal is to cross off all the boxes on your game card in the fewest number of spins.

Total Spins
GAME 1 _____
GAME 2 _____

Game 1

B	B	B	B
R	R	R	R
Y	Y	Y	Y

Extras

B	R	Y

Game 2

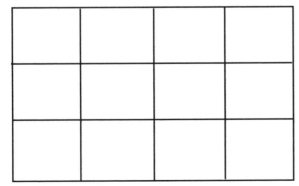

Extras

Spinner Possibilities

1. How would you describe your chances of getting each color with words and numbers?

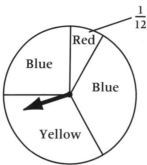

2. Show the chances of getting each color on the probability line below.

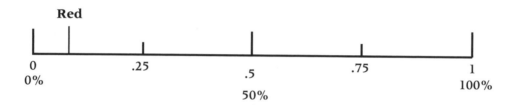

3. How would you make a spinner to meet each pair of conditions listed below? Draw pictures of the spinners.

A. You will spin **yellow** *about* $\frac{1}{3}$ of the time.
   You have the same chances of spinning **red** or **blue**.

B. You will spin **red** *about 50%* of the time.
   Yellow and **blue** are equally likely to be spun.

C. You are *three times* more likely to spin **blue** than **yellow**.
   You will spin **yellow** *about* $\frac{1}{4}$ of the time.

D. The probability of spinning **blue** is 0.
   The probability of spinning **red** is 1.

E. Add your own:_____.

Design Your Own Cover-Up Game

Design a spinner.
Design a spinner with 3-6 parts. Label the parts with the names of foods, sports, or whatever you want.

Fill in the game card for your spinner.
Make a card that gives you a good chance of crossing off the boxes in the *fewest* spins.

Play your game.
Keep a record of the Extras you get in the table below.

Explain why you filled in the game card the way you did.
Use the back of this sheet or a separate sheet.

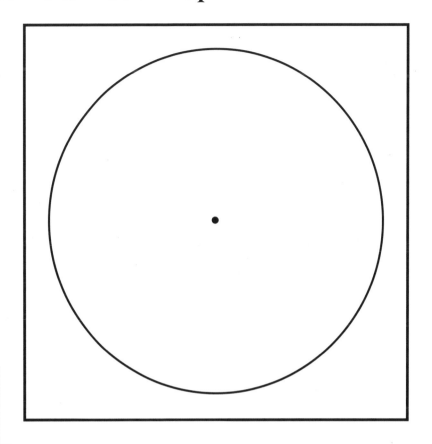

Total Number of Spins	
Predictions	Results

Game Card

Extras

Mystery Spinner Game Rules

Number of Players: 4

Rules:

- Each player gets one clue.

- Players read the clues aloud to the group. They **cannot** show their clues to one another.

- The group needs to draw *one* spinner that matches all the players' clues.

- Label the parts of the spinner with fractions or percents.

- Check to make sure the spinner matches all the clues.

Sample Game

Clues:

A. The spinner has the 4 kinds of prizes. You are likely to win an apple about 50% of the time.

B. You will probably get sunglasses about $\frac{1}{4}$ of the time.

C. In 80 spins, you will probably get a T-shirt about 10 times.

D. You have the same chances of getting a stuffed animal as getting a T-shirt.

Mystery Spinner Games

Game 1

At Pete's Pizza, customers can win a free topping by spinning a spinner. **Pepperoni and sausage** have the same chances of being spun.

Game 1

You will probably get **extra cheese** about $\frac{3}{8}$ of the time.

Game 1

Mushroom is likely to come up about $\frac{1}{8}$ of the time.

Game 1

The chances of getting **sausage** are about 25%.

Game 2

This spinner has four different prizes that you can win. You are likely to win a **pair of socks** about $\frac{1}{4}$ of the time.

Game 2

You are likely to win a **pair of shoelaces** about 50% of the time.

Game 2

The chances of winning **sneakers** are *half* the chances of winning socks.

Game 2

You will probably win a year's supply of soap about $\frac{1}{8}$ of the time.

Game 3

With this spinner, players can win free tickets to four different events. In 100 spins, you are likely to win **movie tickets** about 25 times.

Game 3

You have a 1 out of 4 chance of winning free **baseball tickets**.

Game 3

It is likely that you will win **basketball tickets** about $\frac{1}{6}$ of the time.

Game 3

You are *twice* as likely to win **concert tickets** as basketball tickets.

Mystery Spinner Games

Game 4

Ann's juke-box has a spinner that gives customers a chance of hearing a free song. The probability of getting a jazz song is $\frac{1}{16}$.

Game 4

In 200 spins, you are likely to get a **rap** song 100 times and a **rock** song 50 times.

Game 4

You have the same chances of getting a **country-western** song as a **jazz** song.

Game 4

You are *twice* as likely to get a **rock** song as a **blues** song.

Game 5

At the Chance It Ice Cream store, customers spin a spinner to get a free topping. In 80 spins, you are likely to get **strawberries** 10 times.

Game 5

You have a $\frac{1}{16}$ chance of getting **butterscotch**. **Hot fudge** has the best chance of being spun.

Game 5

You are *three* times as likely to get **whipped cream** as to get **butterscotch**.

Game 5

If you want to get **hot fudge**, you will probably be disappointed about $\frac{6}{16}$ of the time.

Game 6

With this spinner you can win free carnival rides. You will get a **roller coaster** ride about 40% of the time.

Game 6

In 1,000 spins, tilt-a-whirl will come up about 100 times.

Game 6

Your chances of winning a **ferris wheel** ride are *three* times as likely as getting a **tilt-a-whirl** ride.

Game 6

You are *half* as likely to get a **spinning saucers** ride as to get a **roller coaster** ride.

Chance Encounters

Reproducible 14b

Mystery Spinner Games

Game 7 The creatures on the Creepy Crawly game spinner are **snakes, spiders, slugs, bats, and bees.** You are likely to get **snakes about 100 times in 400 spins.**	**Game 7** **Snakes** are *twice* as likely to be spun as **slugs.**	**Game 7** **Slugs and bees** have the same chances of being spun. You have the greatest chance of spinning **spiders.**	**Game 7** You will probably spin things that begin with **B** about $\frac{1}{4}$ of the time and things that begin with **S** about $\frac{3}{4}$ of the time.
Game 8 The five vehicles on this spinner are **bicycle, bus, boat, train, and plane.** You are *four* times as likely to get a **train as a plane.**	**Game 8** You have a 1 in 12 probability of getting a **plane.** The chances of spinning something that begins with **B** are $\frac{7}{12}$.	**Game 8** The chances of getting a **bicycle** are half the chances of getting a **bus.**	**Game 8** In 60 spins, **bus** will probably be spun 20 times.
Game 9 The **Vacation Game** has a spinner with 5 kinds of weather. You will **probably spin hail storm about 10 times out of 160.**	**Game 9** The probability of getting **rain** is *four* times that of getting **hail storm.**	**Game 9** You will probably get **snow** about *half* as often as **rain.**	**Game 9** **Cloudy** has the same chances of being spun as **rain.** You are *five* times as likely to get **sunny as hail storm.**

Chance Encounters

Reproducible 14c

Spinner Design Kit

Cut these spinners into parts that are the sizes you need. Put the parts together to make new spinners. Or, draw your spinners on these templates.

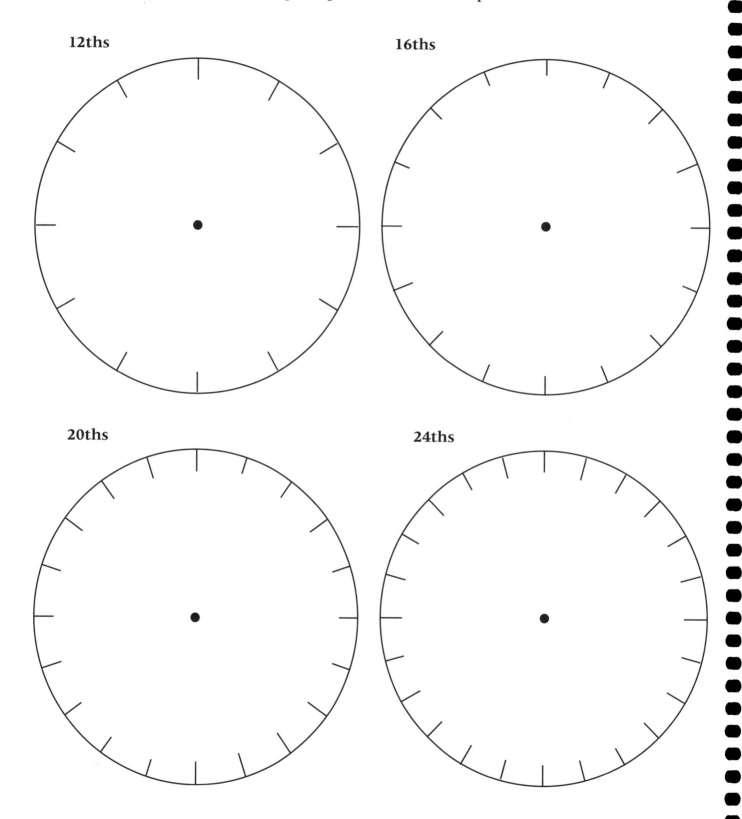

12ths

16ths

20ths

24ths

Spinner Solitaire

For each game, draw a spinner that matches the clues. Label the parts of each spinner with fractions or percents.

Game 1

A. At Sandy's Sandwich shop, customers spin a spinner to get a free sandwich. You are likely to get **turkey** 50% of the time.

B. The chances of getting **tuna fish** are the same as getting **cheese**.

C. You will probably get **cheese** 10 times out of 80 spins.

D. The chances of getting **peanut butter** are about .25.

Game 2

A. This spinner has four kinds of sports equipment you can win. The chances of getting a **basketball** are $\frac{1}{6}$.

B. You are *twice* as likely to get **sneakers** as a **basketball**.

C. You will probably get **skates** about 40 times in 240 spins.

D. The chances of getting a **frisbee** are about .33.

Game 3

A. This spinner has five types of pets that you can win: **goldfish, bird, snake, dog, and cat.** You will get a **goldfish** about 20 times in 160 spins.

B. You are *twice* as likely to get a **bird** as to get a **goldfish**.

C. The chances of getting a **dog** are 3 out of 8.

D. You are *half* as likely to get a **snake** as a **bird**.

E. The chances of getting an animal with four legs are .50.

What's Wrong with These Games?

Figure out what's wrong with the games below. Change the clues to fix the problems.

Game 1

  A. You have the highest chance of winning a bike.

  B. The chances of winning a skateboard are $\frac{1}{16}$.

  C. Car has the same chances as skateboard.

  D. Motorcycle has the same chances as roller blades.

  E. You have a 50% chance of winning roller blades.

Game 2

  A. There are four types of snacks on this spinner.

  B. The chances of winning a bag of popcorn are $\frac{1}{12}$.

  C. You will probably get a free apple 10 times out of 30 spins.

  D. You have the same chances of getting carrots as getting popcorn.

  E. You have the smallest chance of getting pretzels.

Design Your Own Mystery Spinner Game

Spinner Guidelines

- Draw a spinner with 3 – 5 parts.

- Label the spinner parts with the names of foods, music groups, sports, or whatever you want.

- Show the size of each spinner part by labeling it with a fraction or a percent.

Clue Guidelines

- Write at least 4 clues.

- Use a variety of words and numbers to describe the probability of spinning each spinner part.

- Make sure that your clues tell your classmates everything they need to know to draw your spinner.

Tip: Write your clues on a different piece of paper from your spinner. Keep the solution hidden from your classmates.

Unfinished Games

1. Write the missing clues.

This mystery spinner game has a solution spinner but no clues. Write at least 4 clues to describe the spinner.

Use a variety of ways — words and numbers — to describe the probabilities. Do *not* use just one type of clue, like all fractions or all percents.

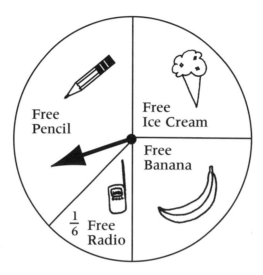

2. Improve these clues.

- What's wrong with the clues listed below? Describe the problems with these clues.

- Write a new version of the clues and draw the solutioin spinner. Make sure to use a variety of ways to describe chances in your clues.

Clues
A. Each part of the spinner has the name of a different sport: soccer, tennis, gymnastics, baseball and basketball.
B. Tennis has a 1 in 3 chance of coming up.
C. Soccer and tennis have the same chances of coming up.
D. Gymnastics has twice as much chance of coming up as tennis.
E. Baseball has twice as much chance of coming up as gymnastics.

Is *Special Sums* Fair?

> **Rules for the Special Sums Game**
>
> Players take turns rolling 2 number cubes. **Add** the two numbers.
>
> Player A gets 1 point if the sum is 1, 2, 3, or 4.
> Player B gets 1 point if the sum is 5, 6, 7, or 8.
> Player C gets 1 point if the sum is 9, 10, 11, or 12.
>
> Play 15 times. (Each player gets 5 turns.) The player with the most points wins.
>
> Note: You can get points on another player's turn. For example, if any player rolls a sum of 10, Player C scores a point.

Guidelines for testing the game

1. Predictions: Before you play, make a prediction and circle it.

FAIR   UNFAIR

Why do you think Special Sums is fair or unfair?

2. Results: Play the game and record the number of points each player gets. Keep track of the number of rolls. The game ends after 15 rolls.

PLAYER A	PLAYER B	PLAYER C

3. Conclusions: Now that you've played the game, circle your conclusion:

FAIR   UNFAIR

Did playing the game change your opinion about whether it is fair or unfair? Why or why not?

Making Outcome Grids

1. **List the ways.** What are all the possible ways that you can make the sums for Player C?   Complete the list below.

Sums	Possible ways of rolling sum with two number cubes
9	4,5 5,4 6,3 3,6
10	
11	
12	

2. **Make an Outcome Grid** for the Special Sums Game. The grid shows all the possible sums you can make when you roll two number cubes. Fill in all the blank boxes.

Numbers on Cube #2

Numbers on Cube #1

	1	2	3	4	5	6
1						
2		4				
3						9
4						
5			8			
6						

3. **Color or code** the grid to show the ways each player can get points. Use a different color or symbol for each player.
   What is each player's probability of getting points?

   Player A : _____   B : _____   C : _____

Change *Special Sums*

The *AllPlay Company* wants you to change the rules of Special Sums to make it fair.

1. Make a grid to show all the possible sums in the Special Sums game.

Numbers on Cube #2

Numbers on Cube #1

	1	2	3	4	5	6
1						
2		4				
3						9
4						
5			8			
6						

2. Write new rules to make the game fair. Use the grid to help you figure out which sums win points for which players. Complete the rules below.

> Players take turns rolling two number cubes. **Add** the two numbers.
>
> Player A gets 1 point when the sums are _____
>
> Player B gets 1 point when the sums are _____
>
> Player C gets 1 point when the sums are _____
>
> The player with the most points after 15 rolls wins. (Each player gets 5 turns.)

3. Color or code the grid to show the ways each player can get a point.

4. Explain why your new game is fair.

5. Extension: Find another way to make the game fair.

100 Tosses

If you toss two number cubes 100 times, how many of each sum will you get?
Conduct an experiment to find out.

Make predictions

Use your outcome grid to answer these questions:

1. Which sum will get you the most?   the least?

2. Which of these bar graphs do you think your results will look most like?
   Why?

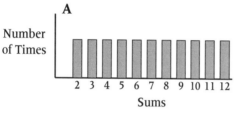

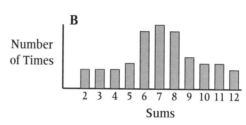

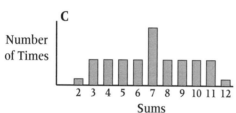

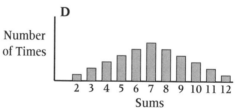

Conduct the experiment and record your results

3. Make a bar graph of your results.

Analyze your results

4. Did you get any surprising results?

5. How do your results compare with the predictions you made from the
   outcome grid?

6. What do you think the results would look like if you did 1,000 trials?   Why?

Fair or Unfair?

1.
Match and Mismatch Game

Materials: Two coins

Rules: Toss both coins.

  Player A gets 1 point if there are 2 Heads or 2 Tails.

  Player B gets 1 point if there is 1 Head and 1 Tail.

The first player to get 7 points wins.

---

2. Two Heads are Better than One Game

Materials: One coin and one number cube

Rules: Flip the coin and roll the number cube.

  Player A gets 1 point if you get Heads and a number   2.

  Player B gets 1 point if you get Tails and a number   4.

The first player to get 7 points wins.

---

3. Odds and Evens Sums Game

Materials: Two number cubes

Rules: Roll both number cubes. Add the two numbers.

  Player A gets 1 point if the sum is even.

  Player B gets 1 point if the sum is odd.

The player with the most points after 15 rolls wins.

---

4. Odds and Evens Products Game

Materials: Two number cubes

Rules: Roll both number cubes. Multiply the two numbers.

  Player A gets 1 point if the product is even.

Fair or Unfair?

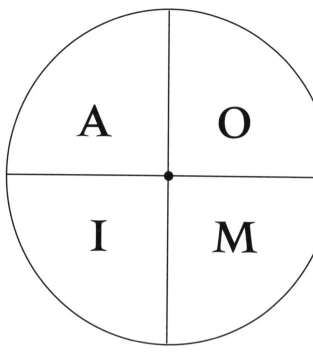

5. Spelling Bee Game

Rules:

Spin the spinners. Try to make a word, like AT or ME. You can reverse the letters.

** Player A gets 1 point when the two letters make a word.

** Player B gets 1 point when the two letters do *not* make a word.

The player with the most points after 15 spins is the winner.

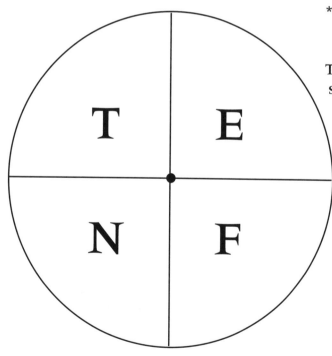

Fair or Unfair?

6. The Music Game

Fill in the spinner:

In 3 of the spinner parts, write the names of music groups that you like. Put one name in each part.

In 2 of the parts, write the names of radio stations that you like. Put one name in each part.

Rules:
Spin the spinner twice.

Player A gets 1 point, if you get a music group and a radio station.

Player B gets 1 point, if you get 2 different music groups or 2 different radio stations.

Player C gets 1 point, if you get the same group twice or same radio station twice.

The first player to get 7 points wins.

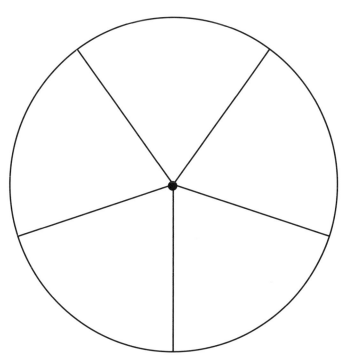

---

7. Hungry and Thirsty Game

Fill in the spinner:

In 6 of the spinner parts, write the names of foods you like or draw pictures of them. Put one food in each part.

In 2 of the parts, write the names of beverages you like or draw pictures of them. Put one beverage in each part.

Rules:
Toss the coin and spin the spinner. On the coin, Heads stands for Hungry and Tails stands for Thirsty.

Player A gets 1 point, if the coin lands on Thirsty and the spinner on a beverage.

Player B gets 1 point, if you get Hungry and a food.

Player C gets 1 point, if you get Hungry and a beverage or Thirsty and a food.

The first player to get 7 points wins.

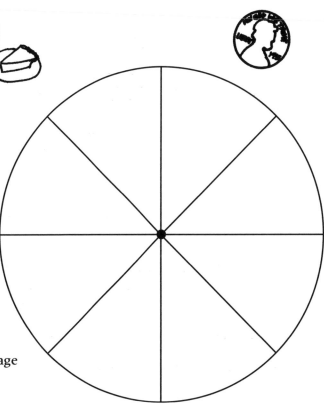

Chance Encounters   *Reproducible 24c*

Fair or Unfair?

8.
Greater Than/Less Than Game

Materials: One number cube and 10 digit cards with the numbers 0-9. You could substitute a 10-sided die for the digit cards.

Rules:

Shuffle the digit cards and then turn one over. Roll the number cube. Make the largest 2-digit number you can.

Player A gets 1 point if the 2-digit number is **less than 35**.
Player B gets 1 point if the 2-digit number is **greater than 70**.
Player C gets 1 point if the 2-digit number is **greater than 35 and less than 70**.

The first player to get 7 points wins.

Tip: Make sure to put the digit card back in the deck and shuffle after each turn.

---

9. The What's the Difference Game

Materials: Divide the digit cards into 1 deck of even numbers, including 0 (0, 2, 4, 6, 8) and 1 deck of odd numbers (1, 3, 5, 7, 9).

Rules:

Shuffle the decks. Turn over one card from each deck. Subtract the smaller number from the larger number.

Player A gets 1 point if the difference is **1**.
Player B gets 1 point if the difference is **5 or 7**.
Player C gets 1 point if the difference is **3 or 9**.

The first player to get 7 points wins.

Tip: Make sure to put the digit cards back in the decks and shuffle after each turn.

Perfect Products

Rules for the Perfect Products Game

Spin both spinners and multiply the numbers.

 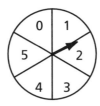

Player A gets 1 point if the product is 0, 10, 20, or 30.

Player B gets 1 point if the product is odd.

Player C gets 1 point if the product is 4, 6, 8 or 12.

Player D gets 1 point if the product is 16, 18 or 24.

1. **Make an outcome grid** for the *Perfect Products* game. Use the space below or a separate sheet of paper.

2. **Color or code** the grid to show the ways each player can get points.

3. **Describe** each player's probability of winning points in 2 ways: fractions, decimals, percents, or ratios.

Player A:_____   Player B:_____

Player C:_____   Player D:_____

4. **Explain** why the game is fair or unfair.

Sneaky Sums

1. Complete the outcome grid for the unfair Sneaky Sums Game.

Rules for the Sneaky Sums Game

Spin both spinners and add the numbers.

Spinner #1   Spinner #2

A gets 1 point when the sum is 4, 5, 6 or 7.

B gets 1 point when the sum is 8, 9 or 10.

C gets 1 point when the sum is 11, 12 or 13.

Outcome Grid for Sneaky Sums

Spinner #2

	0	1	2	3	4	5
4						
5		6				
6						
7					11	
8						

Spinner #1

2. Change the rules to make the game **fair.** Color or code the grid to show how each player can get points.

Your New Rules:

Spin the spinners and add the numbers.

Player A gets 1 point when the sum is _____.

Player B gets 1 point when the sum is _____.

Player C gets 1 point when the sum is _____.

3. Describe each player's probability of getting points in two ways: fractions, decimals, percents, or ratios.

Player A:_____   Player B:_____   Player C:_____

4. Describe how you changed the rules to make the game fair.

5. Extension: Find a different way to make the game fair.

From Numbers to Grids

This sheet lists 6 different probabilities of winning games.

1. Fill in the boxes on the grids to show each probability.

A. $\dfrac{16}{36}$

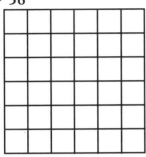

B. 25%

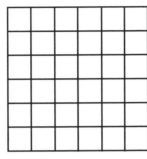

Example

$\dfrac{1}{6}$

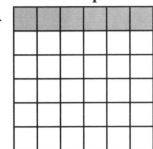

C. 3 out of 4

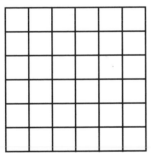

D. $\dfrac{1}{3}$

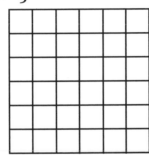

E. .50

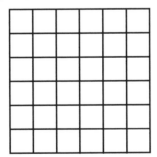

F. 6 out of 18

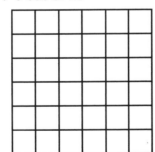

2. Rank the grids from best chances of winning to worst chances of winning. (Best=1)

A_____   B_____   C_____   D_____   E_____   F_____

3. What is the probability of *not* winning for each of the grids?

A_____   B_____   C_____   D_____   E_____   F_____

Rank the Grids

These are probability grids for four different unfair games. If you were Terry, which game would you want to play?

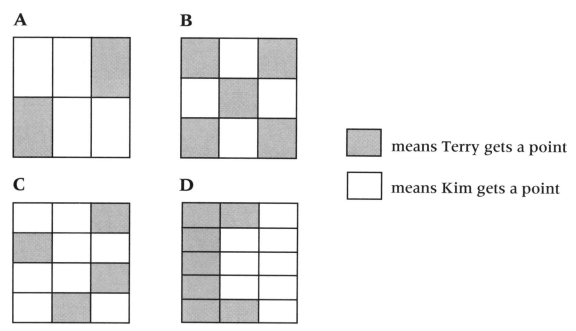

A   **B**

■ means Terry gets a point

□ means Kim gets a point

C   **D**

1. Describe Terry's probability of getting a point in each game in at least two different ways, as fractions, decimals, percents, or ratios.

    A:_____   B:_____

    C:_____   D:_____

2. Rank the grids from "Best for Terry" to "Worst for Terry" (Best =1).

    A_____   B_____   C_____   D_____

3. How did you figure out how to rank the grids?

4. On the other side of this sheet, make a grid that is *better* for Terry than the *second best* game, but *not as good as* the *best* game.

Is This High Scoring Game Fair?

> **Rules for the Super Subtraction Game**
>
> Roll two number cubes. Subtract the smaller number from the larger number.
>
> Player A gets 30 points if the difference is **0 or 5**.
>
> Player B gets 10 points if the difference is **1, 2 or 3**.
>
> Player C gets 45 points if the difference is **4**.
>
> The player with the most points after 18 rolls wins.

1. Make an outcome grid on a separate sheet of paper to figure out each player's probability of scoring points in the **Super Subtraction Game**.

2. Complete the table below.

Players	Probability of scoring points on a turn	Number of times each player is expected to score points in 18 turns	Number of points each player can score on a turn	Expected total number of points in 18 turns
A	$\frac{8}{36}$	4	30	120
B			10	
C			45	

3. Is the game fair or unfair? Why?   If the game is unfair, how would you change the number of points each player can score to make it fair?

4. If player A gets 6 points on a turn, how many points would you give each of the other players to make the game fair? Why?

5. Come up with your own scoring system to make the game fair.

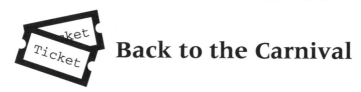

Back to the Carnival

Use what you have learned in Sections 2 and 3 to analyze the Carnival Game from Lesson 1.

1. What are the chances of winning at the *Coin and Cube* booth and the *Teens Only* booth? Describe the probability of winning as fractions, decimals, percents, or ratios.

2. Show your chances of winning at each of the 6 booths (A – F) on the probability line below.

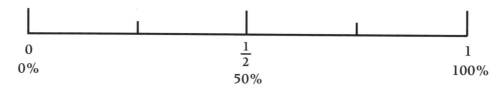

$$0 \qquad\qquad\qquad \frac{1}{2} \qquad\qquad\qquad 1$$

0%   50%   100%

3. The booth owners want to increase the number of tickets players can win on a turn in order to make the booths equally fair. They want players to be likely to win about 24 tickets in 12 turns. How many tickets should each booth give out when a player wins a turn?

   Complete the table below.

Booth	Theoretical probability of winning on 1 turn	Expected number of wins in 12 turns	Number of tickets you can win on a turn	Expected number of tickets in 12 turns
A. Get Ahead	$\frac{1}{2}$ or .5	6	4	24
B. Lucky 3s				
C. Evens or Odds				
D. Pick a Number				
E. Coin and Cube				
F. Teens Only				

4. Extension: Find another way to make the booths equally fair.

Miniature Golf Simulation

Red Yellow	1	2	3	4	5	6
1	Hole in One (1)	Missed by a Mile (5)	Putt, Putt Putt (3)	In the Water (4)	Out of Control (5)	Lost Your Touch (4)
2	Wimpy Putt (3)	Hole in One! (1)	Wimpy Putt (3)	Good Shot! (2)	Perfect Putt (2)	Putt, Putt Putt (3)
3	Lost Your Touch (4)	Stuck under Lighthouse (4)	Hole in One! (1)	Stuck under Lighthouse (4)	Missed by a Mile (5)	Out of Control (5)
4	Out of Control (5)	Sun in Your Eyes (3)	Missed by a Mile (5)	Hole in One! (1)	Putt, Putt Putt (3)	Good Shot! (2)
5	Out of Control (5)	Perfect Putt (2)	Wimpy Putt (3)	Good Shot! (2)	Hole in One! (1)	Perfect Putt (2)
6	In the Water (4)	Good Shot! (2)	Putt, Putt Putt (3)	Sun in Your Eyes (3)	Perfect Putt (2)	Hole in One! (1)

DIRECTIONS

On your turn, roll two different colored number cubes and read the results on the grid. The number in the box shows how many strokes it took to get the ball in the hole. Record that number on your score card.

> For example, if Sal rolls a red 4 and a yellow 2, he would get a Good Shot (2). That means it took 2 strokes to get the ball in the hole. His score is 2.

| Good |
| Shot! |
| (2) |

Hole	Sal's Scores	Ann's Scores
1	2	

Play **18** holes. The player with the *lowest* score is the winner!

Chance Encounters   *Reproducible 31*

Scoresheet

Mini Golf Mania!

PLAYERS

HOLE				
1				
2				
3				
4				
5				
6				
7				
8				
9				
10				
11				
12				
13				
14				
15				
16				
17				
18				
TOTAL				

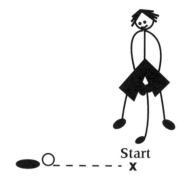

Hole in One: Score 1 pt.

Five tries to get ball in hole:
Score 5 pts.

In miniature golf, *low* scores are better than high scores. The player with the *lowest* number of points after 18 holes wins.

Baseball Simulation

Red Green	1	2	3	4	5	6
1	Home Run!!	Strike OUT	Fly OUT	Single	Single	Ground OUT
2	Ground OUT	Triple	Single	Double	Strike OUT	Fly OUT
3	Fly OUT	Strike OUT	Home Run!!	Double	Fly OUT	Ground OUT
4	Single	Ground OUT	Strike OUT	Ground OUT	Fly OUT	Home Run!!
5	Ground OUT	Single	Triple	Home Run!!	Ground OUT	Strike OUT
6	Fly OUT	Ground OUT	Single	Fly OUT	Triple	Ground OUT

Rules: Draw a baseball diamond on a separate sheet of paper.

- Each player represents a baseball team. On your turn, roll two number cubes and read the grid to find out if your batter gets a hit. (Use chips or small pieces of paper to keep track of your runners on the diamond.)

  Single: all runners advance 1 base   **Double:** all runners advance 2 bases
  Triple: all runners advance 3 bases   **Home Run:** all runners score

- You keep playing until your team gets **3 outs**. Then, it's the other team's turn at bat. An inning is over when both teams have had a turn at bat.

- As you play, record what you get on your scorecard. Don't forget to keep track of the number of runs.

Inning	Team	Outs	Singles	Doubles	Triples	Home Runs	Runs	Total Runs
1	A	|||	|||		||		||	2
	B	|||								1

Chance Encounters   *Reproducible 33*

Baseball Scorecard

Inning	Team	Outs	Singles	Doubles	Triples	Home Runs	Runs	Total Runs per Team
1	A							
	B							
2	A							
	B							
3	A							
	B							
4	A							
	B							
5	A							
	B							
6	A							
	B							
7	A							
	B							
8	A							
	B							
9	A							
	B							

Chance Encounters

Reproducible 34

Data from Actual Miniature Golf Games

Source: Scorecards from a miniature golf course in South Carolina

Total Number of Games Played: 43

Total Number of Holes Played: 774

Average Score: 40.3

Table :

Event	Total Times Each Event Happened in 43 Games (18 holes in each game)	Average Times per Game (18 holes)
Hole-In-One	85	1.9
2 Strokes	477	?
3 Strokes	159	3.7
4 Strokes	49	?
5 Strokes	4	?

Graph of Scores in 43 Actual Games

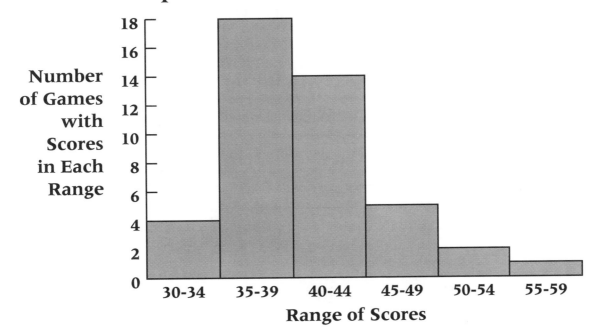

Data from Actual Baseball Games

**Team: Toronto Blue Jays,
1993 season**
**Total Number
of Games Played: 162**

Total Number of At Bats: 5,579
Average Runs per Game: 5.23
Team Batting Average: .279

Table 1: Totals and Averages for Each Event

Event	Total Times Each Event Happened in 162 Games	Average Times Each Event Happened per Game
Single	1,038	6.41
Double	317	?
Triple	42	?
Home Run	159	?
Out (strike out, fly out & ground out)	4,023	24.83

Table 2: Experimental Probabilities of Events

Event	Experimental Probability of Event as a Fraction in 5,579 At Bats	Experimental Probability of Event as a Percentage in 5,579 At Bats
Single	$\frac{1038}{5579}$	19%
Double	$\frac{317}{5579}$	6%
Triple	$\frac{42}{5579}$	?
Home Run	$\frac{159}{5579}$	?
Out (strike out, fly out & ground out)	$\frac{4023}{5579}$	?

Shape Toss

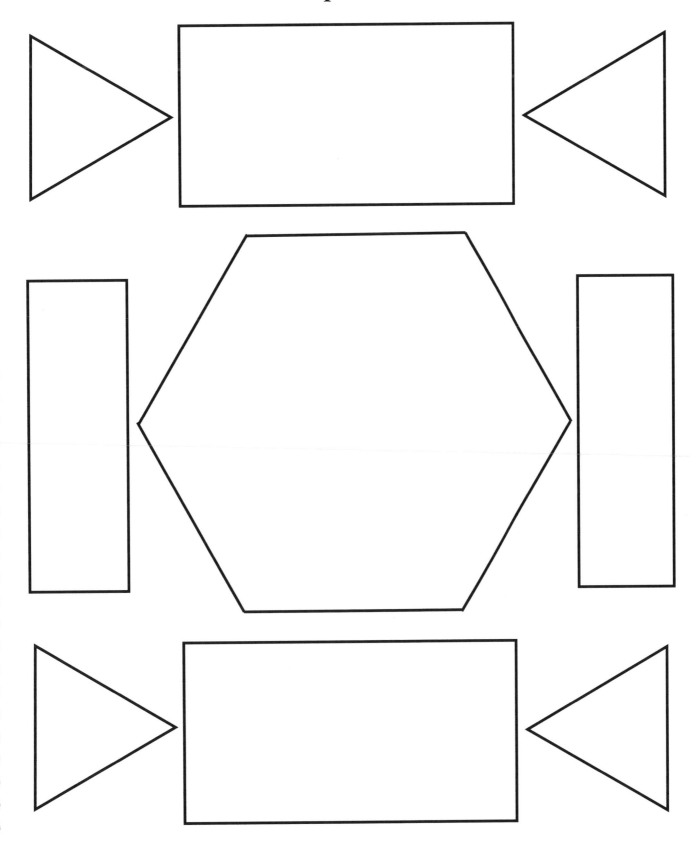

Chance Encounters

Map Toss Game Board

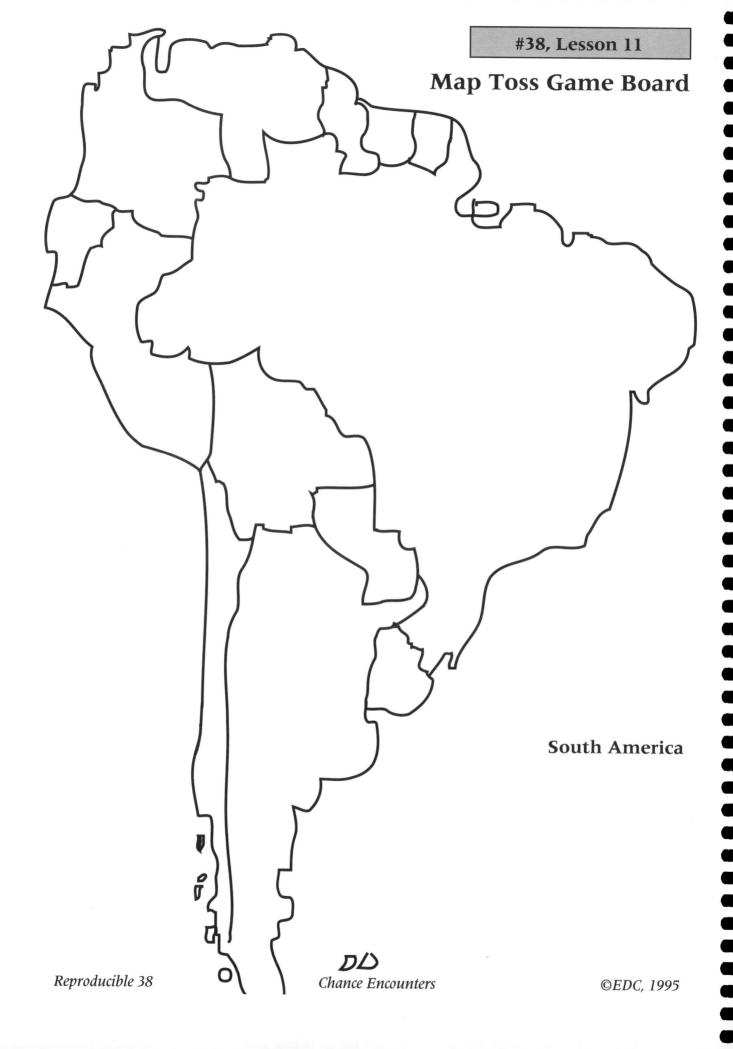

South America

Chance Encounters

Name(s)

Final Project: Design a Simulation Game

What You Need to Do:	Due Date
A. Plan your simulation game. Choose a real-world activity you want to simulate. Describe your ideas and how you will collect data on the *Planning Sheet.*	
B. Collect data on the real-world activity. Display the data you collected and describe how you collected it. Write a summary of what you found out.	
C. Make a probability line. Use your data to rank the likelihood of the real-world events from *least likely* to *most likely.*	
D. Design a grid gameboard for your simulation. Decide which two game pieces (cubes, spinners, etc.) you will use to play your simulation and draw a blank grid with the appropriate number of boxes. For example, use a 36-box grid for two number cubes. Fill in your grid to make a realistic simulation. How many boxes will you give to each event? Color or code the events so that all the boxes for one event have the same color or picture.	
E. Describe the probability of events in your simulation. What are the chances of each event happening in your simulation? Use fractions, percents, decimals, or ratios to describe the probabilities.	
F. Write the rules. What's the goal? How do players score points? When does the game end? You may want to design a score sheet.	
G. Try out your simulation game. Play your simulation at least two times and record the results. Describe what happened when you played. This isn't an accurate test of the simulation, but it will give you a sense of what it's like to play.	
H. Put the pieces of your report together and complete the Cover Sheet. Write a description of your simulation and how you designed it.	

Project Planning Sheet

☐ 1. **Describe the topic.** *Tip:* Pick an activity you know well.
   • What activity are you planning to simulate?
   • What is your experience with the activity you plan to simulate?
   • Why do you think the topic will be interesting to other students?

☐ 2. **List at least 6 different events that might happen in the real activity.**
   Try to come up with events that have a different probability of occurring–
   events that are very likely, likely, unlikely, and very unlikely.

☐ 3. **Describe how you will gather data on your topic.** You need to find out
   the probabilities of different events occurring in the real activity.
   Here are some ways to gather data:
   • Interview people who know a lot about the topic.
   • Look for books that contain statistics on your topic, such as sports almanacs.
   • Keep a record of your own experiences and those of your friends or family.
   • Watch the activity in person or on television.
   • Look in newspapers and magazines.

Final Project Cover Sheet

1. **What is your simulation about?**

2. **How did you collect your real-world data?** (Include the names of your sources.)

3. **What are the probabilities of the real-world events?**
   Show the likelihood of the real-world events on the probability line below.

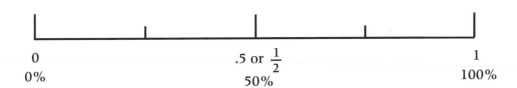

0	.5 or $\frac{1}{2}$	1
0%	50%	100%

4. **What are the probabilities of events in your simulation?**

Events	Number of boxes you gave the event in your simulation grid	Probability of event in your simulation (as a percentage, ratio, fraction or decimal)

Simulation Testing Sheet

Test your classmates' simulations and give them feedback. Remember, your job is to help your classmates improve their games.

Name of the Simulation:_____

1. What do you like about the simulation?

2. What suggestions would you like to give the game designer?

3. How realistic is the simulation?

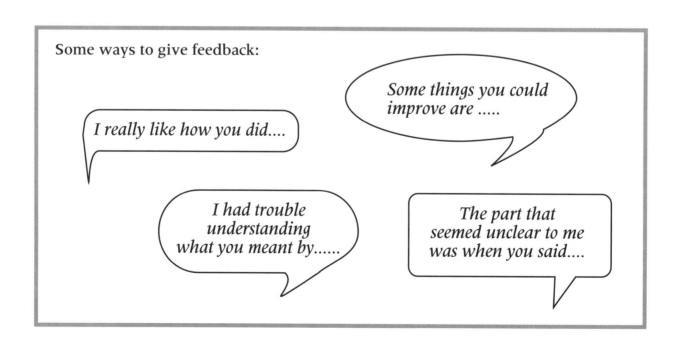

Some ways to give feedback:

I really like how you did....

Some things you could improve are .....

I had trouble understanding what you meant by......

The part that seemed unclear to me was when you said....

Estimada familia:

Nuestra clase pronto empezará una unidad nueva de matemáticas que se llama *Encuentros con la casualidad: probabilidad en juegos y simulaciones*. La unidad se centra en el estudio de temas fundamentales para el estudio de la probabilidad y la estadística, recomendados para los estudiantes de enseñanza media por el Consejo Nacional de Profesores de Matemáticas (National Council of Teachers of Mathematics). Esta unidad también les proporciona a los estudiantes la oportunidad de aplicar y ampliar su conocimiento de los porcentajes, fracciones, decimales y razones.

Durante la unidad, los estudiantes usarán las matemáticas para analizar juegos y simulaciones. Investigarán maneras de mejorar juegos y simulaciones y crearán los suyos propios. Además, los estudiantes investigarán el papel que juega la probabilidad en diferentes situaciones reales, como en los acontecimientos deportivos. Aquí hay algunas de las preguntas sobre las que investigarán los estudiantes:

- ¿Cómo podemos comparar las probabilidades de distintos sucesos?
- ¿Cómo podemos determinar si un juego es justo?
- ¿Cómo podemos determinar la probabilidad de ganar un juego?
- ¿Cómo podemos describir probabilidades de distintas maneras,

  usando fracciones, porcentajes, gráficas y diagramas?
- ¿Cómo podemos diseñar un tablero de juego que simule las

  probabilidades de distintos sucesos, como conseguir un jonrón o fallar con el bate al jugar al béisbol?

Usted puede ayudar a su hijo(a) jugando y discutiendo con él(la) algunos de los juegos de la unidad o sus juegos familiares favoritos. ¿Qué juegos se basan en el azar? ¿Qué juegos les proporcionan a los jugadores mejores oportunidades de ganar? Anime a su hijo(a) a compartir con usted los juegos y simulaciones que él o ella haga, y háblele sobre las maneras en que la probabilidad se usa en la vida diaria.

Juegos de la feria

Boleto

A. Caseta Pase Adelante

Lanza una moneda.

Cara = 1 boleto
Cruz = 0

B. Caseta 3 de la Suerte

Tira un dado.

3 = 1 boleto
1, 2, 4, 5 o 6 = 0

C. Caseta Pares o Impares

Tira un dado.

2, 4 o 6 = 1 boleto
1, 3 o 5 = 0

D. Caseta Elige un Número

Pronostica el número que vas a sacar. Después, tira el dado.

Si la predicción
se cumple = 2 boletos
Si no = 0

E. Caseta Moneda y Dado

Lanza una moneda y tira un dado.

Cruz & 3, 4, 5 o 6 = 1 boleto
Todo lo demás = 0

F. Caseta Sólo Jóvenes

Tira un dado dos veces.
Haz un número de dos dígitos.
(Puedes invertir el orden de los dígitos.)

13, 14, 15 o 16 = 1 boleto
Todo lo demás = 0

Reglas: Los jugadores juegan por turnos. En tu turno, elige la caseta en la que quieres jugar y trata de ganar un boleto. Durante el juego puedes ir a todas las casetas, sólo a algunas, o sólo a una. A ver cuántos boletos puedes ganar en 10 turnos.

Chance Encounters ©EDC, 1995

Nombre(s) _____

Marcador para los Juegos de la feria

Jugador(a) 1

Turno	Caseta (letra)	Boletos
1		
2		
3		
4		
5		
6		
7		
8		
9		
10		
Número total de boletos		
Número de turnos con 0 boletos		

Jugador(a) 2

Turno	Caseta (letra)	Boletos
1		
2		
3		
4		
5		
6		
7		
8		
9		
10		
Número total de boletos		
Número de turnos con 0 boletos		

¿A qué casetas has ido? ¿Por qué?
¿Qué cambiarías si volvieras a jugar?

Mejorar los juegos de la feria

1. Clasifica los Juegos de la feria usando una escala de 1 a 5. Explica por qué has elegido esta clasificación.

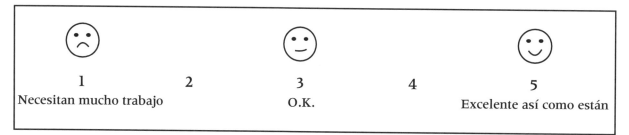

1	2	3	4	5
Necesitan mucho trabajo		O.K.		Excelente así como están

2. Discurre maneras de cambiar los juegos.

   a. ¿Cómo podrías cambiar una caseta o diseñar una nueva para que los jugadores tengan una probabilidad mayor de ganar boletos?

   b. ¿Cómo podrías cambiar una caseta o diseñar una nueva para que los jugadores tengan una probabilidad menor de ganar boletos?

3. Diseña, al menos, una nueva caseta.

Reproducible 4 (Spanish)

Plantillas de gráfica de barra

¿Qué podría ocurrir después de 20 turnos en una de las casetas de la feria?

1. Haz pronósticos.

- ¿Cuántas veces crees que vas a ganar en 20 turnos? ☐

- ¿Cuál crees que va a ser el número más alto de tiradas ganadoras en la clase? ☐

¿El más bajo? ☐

- ¿Cuál crees que va a ser el número más común de tiradas ganadoras? ☐

2. Lleva a cabo el experimento y anota tus resultados.

Con un(a) compañero(a), tira por turnos una moneda o un dado. Anota los resultados en una gráfica de barra como las de abajo. Antes de cada tirada, pronostica lo que vas a sacar. Cuando acabes, colorea las casillas en las que ganarás boletos.

Modelos de gráfica de barra:

Caseta Pase Adelante

| H | H | T | H | T | H | H | T | H | T | H | H | H | H | H | H | T |

☐ Gana   ☐ Pierde (0 Boletos)

Caseta Pares o Impares

| 2 | 3 | 5 | 4 | 4 | 6 | 1 | 2 | 5 | 4 | 1 | 3 | 2 | 5 | 6 | 6 |

Caseta 3 de la Suerte

| 2 | 3 | 5 | 4 | 4 | 6 | 1 | 2 | 5 | 4 | 1 | 3 | 2 | 5 | 3 | 6 | 5 | 4 |

	Sus resultados	Resultados de la clase
Número total de tiradas ganadoras		
Mayor número de tiradas ganadoras consecutivas		
Número más alto de tiradas ganadoras en la clase		
Número más bajo de tiradas ganadoras en la clase		
Número más común de tiradas ganadoras(moda)		

Informe incompleto

Adrianna y Erik han hecho un experimento con un dado numerado, pero no han acabado de escribir su informe. Esto es lo que escribieron:

Tiramos un dado 40 veces para ver cuántos números pares e impares obteníamos. El dado está numerado con los números 1, 2, 3, 4, 5 y 6.

Nosotros pronosticamos que obtendríamos unos 20 números pares y unos 20 impares.

Cuando lanzamos el dado, anotamos una 0 si obteníamos un número impar y una E si obteníamos uno par.

O	O	E	E	O	O	O	O	O	O
O	O	E	E	O	O	E	E	E	O
O	E	E	O	O	O	O	E	O	E
O	E	E	O	E	E	O	E	O	O

Acaba de escribir el informe.

1. Con los resultados, haz una tabla, un gráfico de frecuencia o una gráfica de barra en una hoja de papel aparte.

2. ¿Qué fracción o porcentaje de las 40 tiradas corresponde a números impares? ¿A números pares? (Esto se llama probabilidad experimental).

    Probabilidad experimental de obtener un número impar:_____

    Probabilidad experimental de obtener un número par:_____

3. ¿Qué resultados crees que habrían obtenido Adrianna y Erik si hubieran tirado el dado 1.000 veces? ¿Por qué?

4. ¿Cuántas tiradas crees que serán necesarias para obtener aproximadamente **80 números pares**? ¿Por qué?

¿Qué probabilidad tiene?

1. ¿Qué probabilidad hay de que diferentes eventos ocurran en un día típico de escuela?

   Aquí hay algunos eventos que podrían ocurrir durante un día de escuela. Colócalos ordenadamente en una línea de probabilidad, *de menos probable a más probable.*

   A. Llegar a la escuela puntualmente.　　B. Tener un ejercicio de evacuación.

   C. Recibir tarea.　　　　　　　　　　D. Comerte un sandwich en el almuerzo.

   E. Que falte alguien en tu clase.　　　F. Ver a una famosa estrella cinematográfica.

   G. Ver a alguien con zapatillas.　　　H. Ir al gimnasio.

   I. Añade tu propio evento:_____.

   J. Añade tu propio evento:_____.

Línea de probabilidad

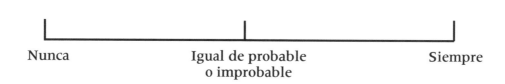

Nunca　　　　　　　　Igual de probable　　　　　　　　Siempre
　　　　　　　　　　　　o improbable

2. Para cada uno de los siguientes, nombra por lo menos *dos* eventos reales que:

   a. **Definitivamente** pasarán mañana　　b. **Probablemente** pasarán mañana

   c. **Probablemente no** pasarán mañana　　d. **Nunca** pasarán mañana

Chance Encounters ©EDC, 1995

¡Ojalá nieve!

El anuncio de abajo es un anuncio auténtico de un periódico de Massachusetts. Léelo y responde a las siguientes preguntas.

Let It Snow!
YOU'LL RECEIVE A
100% REFUND!
ALL PAID IN FULL PURCHASES PICKED UP
BETWEEN NOV. 5 AND DEC. 24, 1993
WILL BE 100% REFUNDED* IF IT SNOWS
3 INCHES OR MORE BETWEEN 6 PM AND
MIDNIGHT ON NEW YEAR'S EVE.
Come in for full details.
Let it Snow! Let it Snow!

Our spectacular selection of fine jewelry includes the latest styles in earrings, gold from Italy, fine diamond and colored gemstone jewelry, designer "one of a kind" pieces, and cultured pearls, priced to fit your budget. Shop early for the best selection.

* Sales tax not refundable.

Carol The Gold Lady, Ltd.
Fine Jewelry
109 Dalby Street, Newton (off Watertown St.)
Ample Free Parking Layaways Accepted
Hours: Tues., Wed., Sat. 10–6; Thurs. & Fri. 10–9 Closed Sun. & Mon.

©1993 Carol L. Bartolomucci

¡Ojalá nieve!
¡Usted recibirá un REEMBOLSO del 100!
TODAS LAS COMPRAS TOTAL MENTE
ABONADAS QUE SE RECOJAN ENTRE EL 5 DE
NOV. Y EL 24 DE DIC. SERÁN REEMBOLSADAS
AL 100* SI CAEN 3 PULGADAS O MÁS DE NIEVE
ENTRE LAS 6 DE LA TARDE Y MEDIANOCHE EN
NOCHEVIEJA.

Venga y conozca los detalles.
¡Que nieve! ¡Que nieve!

1. ¿Crees que esto es un buen negocio? ¿Por qué sí o por qué no?

2. Si este anuncio apareciera en tu área, ¿cómo podrías obtener información para averiguar tus probabilidades de conseguir un reembolso? ¿Qué tipo de información querrías?

3. ¿Cuáles crees que serán tus probabilidades de conseguir un reembolso?

4. ¿En qué zona de los Estados Unidos tendrás más probabilidades de conseguir un reembolso? ¿Menos probabilidades?

5. Diseña tu propio anuncio con factores de probabilidad.

El juego de Rellenar

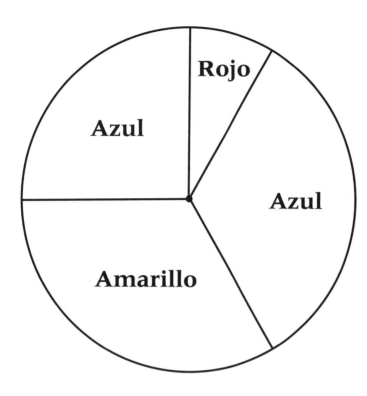

Cómo jugar:
Cuando obtengas un color, pon una X en una de las casillas con ese color que tiene tu tarjeta de juego. Si no necesitas ese color, se cuenta como extra. Pon una marca en la Tabla de Extras.

El juego acaba cuando pones X's en todas las casillas de tu tarjeta de juego.

El objetivo es rellenar todas las casillas en tu tarjeta de juego en el menor número de giros.

Total giros

JUEGO 1 _____

JUEGO 2 _____

Juego 1

B	B	B	B
R	R	R	R
Y	Y	Y	Y

Extras

B	R	Y

Juego 2

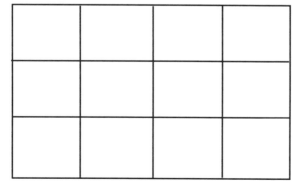

Extras

Posibilidades de la rueda giratoria

1. ¿Cómo describirías con palabras y números la probabilidad que tienes de obtener cada color?

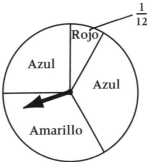

2. Muestra la probabilidad de obtener cada color en la línea de probabilidad de abajo.

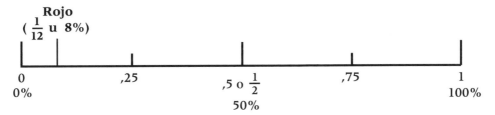

3. ¿Cómo conseguirías que una rueda giratoria cumpliera cada par de condiciones enumeradas abajo? Haz dibujos de las ruedas giratorias.

   A. Al girar la rueda, obtendrás **amarillo** *aproximadamente* $\frac{1}{3}$ de las veces.
   Tienes las mismas oportunidades de obtener **rojo** o **azul**.

   B. Al girar, obtendrás **rojo** *aproximadamente* el 50% de las veces.
   Al girar la rueda, **amarillo** y **azul** tienen las mismas probabilidades de salir.

   C. Al girar, tienes *tres veces* más probabilidades de obtener **azul** que **amarillo**.
   Al girar, obtendrás **amarillo** *aproximadamente* $\frac{1}{4}$ de las veces.

   D. Al girar, la probabilidad de obtener **azul** es 0.
   Al girar, la probabilidad de obtener **rojo** es 1.

   E. Añade la tuya propia:_____.

Diseña tu propio juego de Rellenar

Diseña una rueda giratoria.
Diseña una rueda giratoria que tenga 3-6 partes. Nombra las partes con nombres de alimentos, deportes, o lo que quieras.

Rellena la tarjeta de juego para tu rueda giratoria.
Haz una tarjeta que te dé la oportunidad de rellenar las casillas en *el menor* número de vueltas posible.

Juega a tu juego.
Mantén un registro de los Extras que consigues en la tabla de abajo.

Explica por qué has rellenado la tarjeta de juego en la manera que lo has hecho.
Usa el reverso de esta hoja o una hoja aparte.

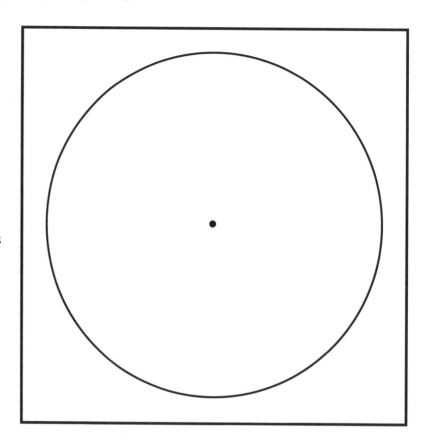

Total número de vueltas	
Pronósticos	Resultados

Tarjeta de juego

Extras

Reglas del juego de la Rueda Misteriosa

Número de jugadores: 4

Reglas:

- Cada jugador(a) recibe una pista.

- Los jugadores leen las pistas en voz alta a los miembros del grupo. **No pueden** mostrarse sus pistas uno a otro.

- El grupo necesita dibujar *una* rueda giratoria que cumpla con todas las pistas de los jugadores.

- Marca las partes de la rueda con fracciones o porcentajes.

- Comprueba para asegurarte de que la rueda se ajusta a todas las pistas.

Juego de muestra

Pistas:

A. La rueda tiene las 4 clases de premios. Puedes ganar una manzana el 50% de las veces, aproximadamente.

B. Probablemente conseguirás las gafas de sol $\frac{1}{4}$ de las veces, aproximadamente.

C. En 80 giros, probablemente conseguirás una camiseta unas diez veces.

D. Tienes las mismas probabilidades de conseguir un animal de peluche que una camiseta.

Juegos de la Rueda Misteriosa

Juego 1

En Pete's Pizza, los clientes pueden ganar un ingrediente gratis al girar una rueda giratoria. **Pepperoni y salchicha** tienen las mismas probabilidades de salir.

Juego 2

En esta rueda giratoria puedes ganar cuatro premios diferentes. Es muy probable que ganes un **par de medias** $\frac{1}{4}$ de las veces.

Juego 3

Con esta rueda giratoria, los jugadores pueden ganar entradas gratis para cuatro eventos diferentes. En 100 giros, es muy probable que ganes **entradas para el cine 25** veces.

Juego 1

Probablemente conseguirás **queso adicional** $\frac{3}{8}$ de las veces, aproximadamente.

Juego 2

Es muy probable que ganes un **par de cordones de zapatos** aproximadamente el 50% de las veces.

Juego 3

La probabilidad que tienes de ganar **entradas gratis para el béisbol** es de 1 en 4.

Juego 1

Champiñones saldrá seguramente $\frac{1}{8}$ de las veces.

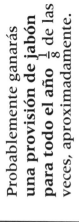

Juego 2

La probabilidad de ganar **zapatillas de deporte** es la mitad de la de ganar **medias.**

Juego 3

Es muy probable que ganes **entradas para el baloncesto** aproximadamente $\frac{1}{6}$ de las veces.

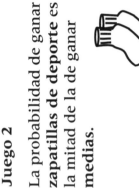

Juego 1

Las probabilidades de sacar **salchicha** son aproximadamente del 25%.

Juego 2

Probablemente ganarás **una provisión de jabón para todo el año** $\frac{1}{8}$ de las veces, aproximadamente.

Juego 3

Tienes el *doble* de probabilidades de ganar **entradas para un concierto** que de ganar **entradas para el baloncesto.**

Juegos de la Rueda Misteriosa

Juego 4 El giradiscos de Ann tiene una rueda giratoria que les proporciona a los clientes la oportunidad de escuchar una canción gratis. La probabilidad de obtener una canción de jazz es de $\frac{1}{16}$.	**Juego 4** En 200 vueltas, seguramente obtendrás 100 veces una canción de rap y 50 veces una canción de rock.	**Juego 4** Tienes la misma probabilidad de sacar una canción de country-**western** que de sacar una canción de jazz.	**Juego 4** Tienes el *doble* de oportunidades de sacar una canción de rock que una canción de blues.
Juego 5 En la heladería Prueba tu Suerte, los clientes giran una rueda giratoria para obtener un ingrediente gratis. En 80 vueltas, seguramente conseguirás fresas 10 veces.	**Juego 5** Tienes una probabilidad de $\frac{1}{16}$ de obtener **caramelo. Chocolate caliente** tiene la mayor probabilidad.	**Juego 5** La probabilidad de obtener **crema batida** es *tres veces* mayor que la de obtener caramelo.	**Juego 5** Si quieres obtener **chocolate caliente**, seguramente te desilusionarás $\frac{6}{16}$ de las veces, aproximadamente.
Juego 6 Con esta rueda giratoria puedes ganar viajes gratis en el parque de atracciones. Conseguirás un viaje en la **montaña rusa** el 40% de las veces, aproximadamente.	**Juego 6** En 1.000 giros, el **balancín saldrá** unas 100 veces.	**Juego 6** Tu probabilidad de ganar un viaje en la **noria** es *tres veces* mayor que la de conseguir un viaje en el **balancín**.	**Juego 6** Tienes la *mitad* de probabilidades de conseguir un viaje en los **platillos volantes** que de conseguirlo en la **montaña rusa**.

Juegos de la Rueda Misteriosa

Juego 7

Las criaturas de la rueda giratoria del juego Lúgubre e Inquietante son **serpientes, arañas, babosas, murciélagos y abejas.** Seguramente obtendrás **serpientes** 100 veces en 400 giros, aproximadamente.

Juego 8

Los cinco vehículos en esta rueda giratoria son: **una bicicleta, un autobús, un bote, un tren y un avión.** La probabilidad de que obtengas un **tren** es *cuatro* veces mayor que la de obtener un **avión.**

Juego 9

El Juego de la Vacación tiene una rueda giratoria con cinco clases de clima. Probablemente obtendrás **tormenta de granizo** unas 10 veces en 160 giros.

Juego 7

Al girar la rueda, **serpientes** seguramente saldrá el *doble* de veces que **babosas.**

Juego 8

Tienes una probabilidad de 1 en 12 de conseguir un **avión.** Las probabilidades de obtener algo que empiece por **B** son $\frac{3}{12}$.

Juego 9

La probabilidad de obtener **lluvia** es *cuatro* veces mayor que la de obtener **tormenta de granizo.**

Juego 7

Babosas y abejas tienen las mismas probabilidades de salir. La mayor probabilidad al girar la rueda corresponde a las **arañas.**

Juego 8

Las probabilidades de obtener una **bicicleta** son la *mitad* de las de obtener un **autobús.**

Juego 9

Probablemente obtendrás **nieve** la mitad de las veces que **lluvia,** aproximadamente.

Juego 7

Conseguirás algo con alas $\frac{1}{4}$ de las veces y algo sin alas $\frac{3}{4}$ de las veces.

Juego 8

En 60 giros, **autobús** probablemente saldrá 20 veces.

Juego 9

Nuboso tiene las mismas probabilidades de salir que **lluvia.** La probabilidad de que te salga **soleado** es *cinco* veces mayor que la de **tormenta de granizo.**

Equipo para el diseño de ruedas giratorias

Recorta estas ruedas giratorias en partes del tamaño que necesites. Junta las partes
para hacer nuevas ruedas giratorias, o dibuja tus ruedas giratorias en estas plantillas.

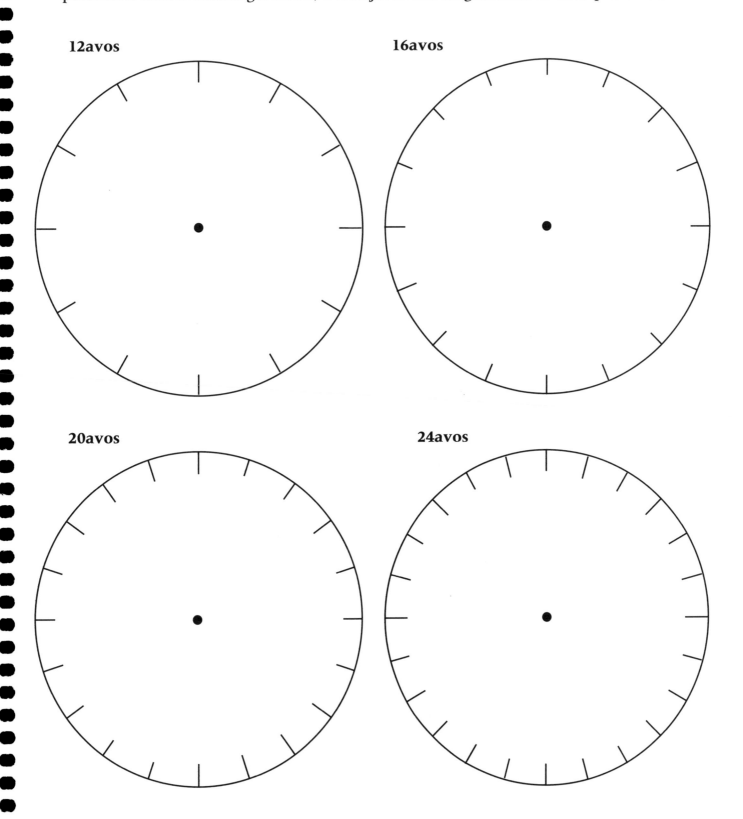

12avos

16avos

20avos

24avos

Solitario de la Rueda Misteriosa

Para cada juego, dibuja una rueda giratoria siguiendo las pistas dadas. Nombra las partes de cada rueda giratoria con fracciones o porcentajes.

Juego 1

A. En la bodega de Sandy los clientes giran una rueda giratoria para conseguir un sandwich gratis. Seguramente obtendrás **pavo** el 50% de las veces.

B. Las probabilidades de obtener **atún** son las mismas que las de obtener **queso**.

C. Seguramente conseguirás **queso** 10 veces de cada 80.

D. La probabilidad de conseguir **mantequilla de cacahuete** es aproximadamente ,25.

Juego 2

A. Con esta rueda giratoria puedes ganar cuatro clases de material deportivo. La probabilidad de obtener una **pelota de baloncesto** es $\frac{1}{6}$.

B. La probabilidad de conseguir **zapatillas** es el *doble* que la de conseguir una **pelota de baloncesto**.

C. Seguramente, conseguirás **patines** 40 veces en 240 giros, aproximadamente.

D. La probabilidad de conseguir un **disco volador** *(frisbee)* es del ,33.

Juego 3

A. En esta rueda giratoria puedes ganar cinco clases de mascotas: **carpa dorada, pájaro, serpiente, perro y gato**. Conseguirás una **carpa dorada** 20 veces en 160 giros.

B. Tienes el *doble* de probabilidades de conseguir un **pájaro** que una **carpa dorada**.

C. La probabilidad de conseguir un **perro** es de 3 de cada 8.

D. La probabilidad de que consigas una **serpiente** es la *mitad* de la probabilidad de que consigas un **pájaro**.

E. La probabilidad de conseguir un animal de cuatro patas es ,50.

¿Qué problema tienen estos juegos?

Descubre cuál es el problema en los juegos que vienen a continuación. Cambia las pistas para corregir los problemas.

Juego 1

A. Tienes la mayor probabilidad de ganar una bicicleta.

B. La probabilidad de ganar una tabla de patinar *(skateboard)* es de $\frac{1}{16}$.

C. Carro tiene las mismas probabilidades que tabla de patinar.

D. Motocicleta tiene las mismas probabilidades que patines de ruedas.

E. Tienes una probabilidad del 50% de ganar unos patines de ruedas.

Juego 2

A. Hay cuatro tipos de meriendas en esta rueda giratoria.

B. La probabilidad de ganar una bolsa de palomitas de maíz *(popcorn)* es de $\frac{1}{12}$.

C. Seguramente conseguirás una manzana gratis 10 veces en 30 giros.

D. Tienes las mismas probabilidades de conseguir zanahorias que de conseguir palomitas de maíz.

E. Los *pretzels* tienen la probabilidad menor.

Instrucciones para rueda giratoria con solución

Instrucciones para construir una rueda giratoria con la solución

- Dibuja una rueda giratoria que tenga 3-5 partes.

- Nombra las partes de la rueda giratoria con nombres de alimentos, grupos musicales, deportes o lo que tú quieras.

- Muestra el tamaño de cada parte de la rueda giratoria y nómbralo con una fracción o un porcentaje.

Instrucciones para las pistas

- Escribe un mínimo de 4 pistas.

- Usa distintas palabras y números para describir la probabilidad de obtener una parte de la rueda giratoria.

- Asegúrate de que tus pistas les proporcionan a tus compañeros(a) de clase todo lo que necesitan saber para dibujar la rueda giratoria.

Consejo: Escribe tus pistas en una hoja de papel aparte (no uses la misma hoja que has usado para la rueda giratoria). No les muestres la solución a tus compañeros(as) de clase.

Juegos incompletos

1. Escribe las pistas que faltan.

La rueda giratoria de este juego de misterio tiene la solución, pero no tiene pistas. Escribe un mínimo de 4 pistas para describir la rueda giratoria.

Describe las probabilidades de maneras distintas, usando palabras y números. *No* uses un solo tipo de pista (todo fracciones o todo porcentajes).

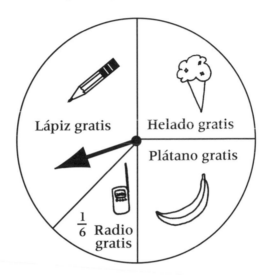

2. Mejora estas pistas.

- ¿Qué problemas tienen las pistas enumeradas abajo? Descríbelos.

- Escribe una nueva versión de las pistas y dibuja la rueda giratoria con la solución. Asegúrate de describir las probabilidades en tus pistas de distintas maneras.

Pistas

A. Cada parte de esta rueda giratoria tiene el nombre de un deporte diferente: fútbol (soccer), tenis, gimnasia, béisbol y baloncesto.

B. Tenis tiene 1 probabilidad de salir de cada 3.

C. Fútbol y tenis tienen las mismas probabilidades de salir.

D. Gimnasia tiene el doble de probabilidades que tenis.

E. Béisbol tiene el doble de probabilidades que gimnasia.

¿Es justo Sumas Especiales?

Reglas para el juego de las Sumas Especiales

Los jugadores tiran por turnos dos dados numerados. **Suma** los dos números.

El(la) jugador(a) A obtiene un punto si la suma es **1, 2, 3 o 4.**
El(la) jugador(a) B obtiene un punto si la suma es **5, 6, 7 o 8.**
El(la) jugador(a) C obtiene un punto si la suma es **9, 10, 11 o 12.**

Jueguen 15 veces (cada jugador(a) recibe 5 turnos). El(la) jugador(a) con más puntos gana.

Nota:

Puedes obtener puntos en el turno de otro jugador. Por ejemplo, si cualquier jugador(a) saca una suma de 10, el(la) jugador(a) C obtiene

Pautas para probar el juego

1. **Pronósticos:** Antes de jugar, haz un pronóstico y rodéalo con un círculo. ¿Te parece que Sumas Especiales es justo o injusto? ¿Por qué?

JUSTO   INJUSTO

2. **Resultados:** Juega al juego y apunta el número de puntos que obtiene cada jugador(a). Apunta el número de tiradas. El juego se acaba después de 15 tiradas.

JUGADOR(A) A	JUGADOR(A) B	JUGADOR(A) C

3. **Conclusiones:** Ahora que ya has jugado, rodea con un círculo tu conclusión:

JUSTO   INJUSTO

Jugar a este juego, ¿te ha hecho cambiar de opinión sobre si este juego es justo o injusto? ¿Por qué sí o por qué no?

Nombre(s) _____

Hacer cuadrículas de resultados

1. Enumera las maneras. ¿De cuántas maneras puedes hacer las sumas para el(la) jugador(a) C? Completa la lista de abajo.

Sumas	Posibilidades de suma al tirar dos dados numerados
9	4,5 5,4 6,3 3,6
10	
11	
12	

2. Haz una cuadrícula del resultado para el juego de las Sumas Especiales. La cuadrícula muestra todas las sumas posibles que puedes obtener al tirar dos dados numerados. Llena todos los cuadros en blanco.

Números en dado 2

	1	2	3	4	5	6
1						
2		4				
3						9
4						
5			8			
6						

Números en dado 1

3. Asígnale un código o colorea la cuadrícula para mostrar las maneras en que cada jugador(a) puede obtener puntos. Usa un color o símbolo diferente para cada jugador(a). ¿Qué probabilidad tiene cada jugador de obtener puntos?

Jugador(a) A : _____   B : _____   C : _____

Cambia Sumas Especiales

La Compaña Todojuego quiere que cambies las reglas para que Sumas Especiales sea un juego justo.

1. **Haz una cuadrícula** para mostrar todas las sumas posibles en el juego Sumas Especiales.

Números en dado 2

	1	2	3	4	5	6
1						
2		4				
3						9
4						
5			8			
6						

Números en dado 1

2. **Escribe nuevas reglas** para hacer el juego justo. Usa la cuadrícula para calcular qué sumas debes darle a cada jugador(a). Completa las reglas de abajo.

> Los jugadores tiran dos dados numéricos por turnos. **Suma** los dos números.
>
> El(la) jugador(a) **A** obtiene un punto cuando la suma es _____
>
> El(la) jugador(a) **B** obtiene un punto cuando la suma es _____
>
> El(la) jugador(a) **C** obtiene un punto cuando la suma es _____
>
> El(la) jugador(a) que obtiene más puntos en 15 tiradas, gana. (Cada jugador(a) tira 5 veces.)

3. **Colorea o aplícale** un código a la cuadrícula para mostrar cómo puedconseguir un punto cada jugador(a).

4. **Explica** por qué tu nuevo juego es justo.

5. **Extensión:** Halla otra manera de hacer justo este juego .

100 Tiradas

Si tiras 100 veces dos dados, ¿cuántas veces obtendrás cada suma? Realiza un experimento para averiguarlo.

Haz un pronóstico

Usa los resultados de tu cuadrícula para responder a estas preguntas:

1. ¿Qué suma crees que obtendrás más a menudo? ¿Menos?

2. ¿A cuál de estas gráficas de barra crees que se parecerán más tus resultados? ¿Por qué?

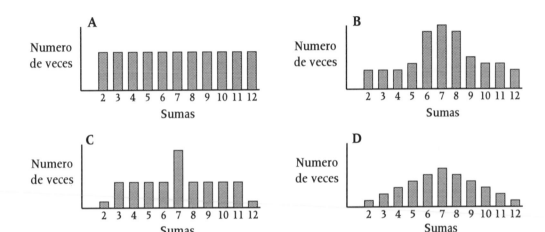

Realiza el experimento y anota tus resultados

3. Haz una gráfica de barra de tus resultados en una hoja de papel aparte.

Analiza tus resultados

4. ¿Has obtenido algún resultado sorprendente?

5. ¿Cómo se comparan tus resultados con los pronósticos que hiciste basándote en los de la cuadrícula?

6. ¿Qué resultados crees que obtendrás si lo hicieras con 1.000 tiradas? ¿Por qué?

¿Justo o injusto?

1. Juego Dos Iguales o Una de Cada

Materiales: dos monedas

Reglas: lanza ambas monedas.

El(la) jugador(a) A obtiene 1 punto si saca 2 caras o 2 cruces.

El(la) jugador(a) B obtiene 1 punto si saca 1 cara y 1 cruz.

Gana el primer jugador que obtenga 7 puntos.

---

2. Dos Caras Son Mejor que un Juego.

Materiales: una moneda y un dado

Reglas: lanza la moneda y tira el dado.

El(la) jugador(a) A obtiene 1 punto si tú sacas cara y un número   2.

El(la) jugador(a) B obtiene 1 punto si tú sacas cruz y un número   4.

Gana el primer jugador que obtenga 7 puntos.

---

3. Juego de las Sumas Pares e Impares

Materiales: dos dados

Reglas: tira ambos dados. Suma los dos números.

El(la) jugador(a) A obtiene 1 punto si la suma es par.

El(la) jugador(a) B obtiene 1 punto si la suma es impar.

Gana el(la) jugador(a) que tenga más puntos después de 15 tiradas.

---

4. Juego del Producto Par o Impar

Materiales: dos dados

Reglas: tira los dos dados. Multiplica los dos números.

El(la) jugador(a) A obtiene 1 punto si el producto es par.

El(la) jugador(a) B obtiene 1 punto si el producto es impar.

¿Justo o injusto?

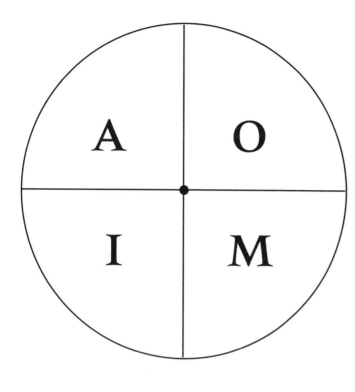

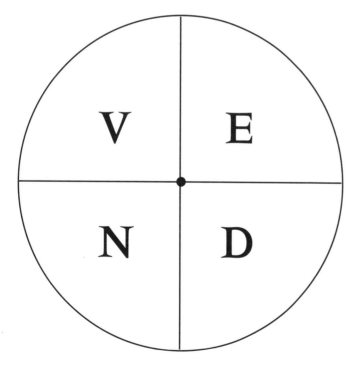

5. El juego del ABCdario

Reglas:

Gira las ruedas giratorias. Trata de construir una palabra, como VA o NO. Puedes invertir las letras.

** El(la) jugador(a) A obtiene un punto cuando las dos letras forman una palabra.

** El(la) jugador(a) B obtiene un punto cuando las dos letras no forman una palabra.

Gana el jugador(a) que obtenga más puntos después de 15 giros.

¿Justo o injusto?

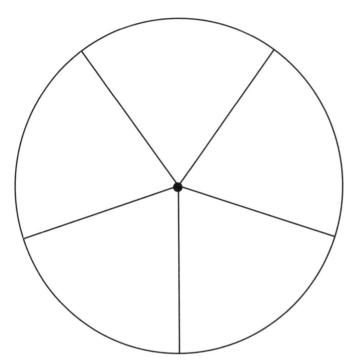

6. El juego de La Música

Rellena la rueda giratoria:

en 3 de las partes de la rueda giratoria, escribe los nombres de grupos musicales que te gustan. Pon un nombre en cada parte.

En dos de las partes, escribe los nombres de emisoras de radio que te gustan. Pon un nombre en cada parte.

Reglas:
gira dos veces la rueda giratoria.

El(la) jugador(a) A consigue un punto si tú obtienes un grupo musical y una emisora de radio.

El(la) jugador(a) B consigue un punto si tú obtienes 2 grupos musicales diferentes o dos emisoras de radio diferentes.

El(la) jugador(a) C consigue un punto si tú obtienes el mismo grupo dos veces o la misma emisora dos veces.

El primer jugador que consiga 7 puntos, gana.

---

7. Juego del Hambriento y Sediento.

Rellena la rueda giratoria:

En 6 de las partes de la rueda giratoria, escribe los nombres de alimentos que te gustan, o haz un dibujo que los represente.

En dos de las partes, escribe los nombres de bebidas que te gusten, o haz un dibujo que las represente. Pon una bebida en cada parte.

Reglas:
lanza la moneda y gira la rueda giratoria. En la moneda, **cara** significa **alimento** y **cruz** significa **bebida**.

El(la) jugador(a) A consigue un punto si en la moneda sale cruz y en la rueda giratoria sale una bebida.

El(la) jugador(a) B consigue un punto si sale cara y un alimento.

El(la) jugador(a) C consigue un punto si sale cara y una bebida, o sediento y un alimento.

El primer jugador que consiga 7 puntos, gana.

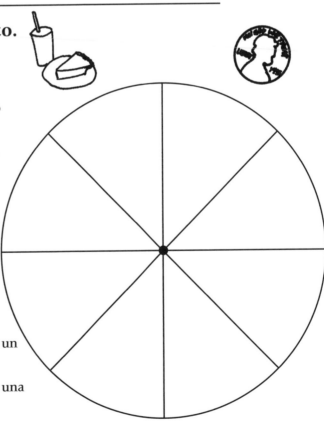

¿Justo o Injusto?

8. Juego Mayor que/Menor que

Materiales: un dado y 10 cartas con números del 0 al 9. Puedes sustituir las cartas por un dado de 10 caras.

Reglas:

baraja las cartas y vuelve una con el número hacia arriba. Tira el dado. Haz el número de dos dígitos más grande que puedas.

El(la) jugador(a) A obtiene 1 punto si el número de dos dígitos es **menor que 35**.
El(la) jugador(a) B obtiene 1 punto si el número de dos dígitos es **mayor que 70**.
El(la) jugador(a) C obtiene 1 punto si el número de dos dígitos es **mayor que 35 y menor que 70**.

El primer jugador que consiga 7 puntos, gana.

Consejo: devuelve la carta al montón y baraja después de cada turno.

---

9. Juego ¿Cuál Es la Diferencia?

Materiales: divide las cartas numéricas en un montón de números pares, incluido el 0 (0, 2, 4, 6, 8) y un montón de números impares (1, 3, 5, 7, 9).

Reglas:

baraja los montones. Dale la vuelta a una cara de cada montón. Sustrae el número menor al número mayor.

El(la) jugador(a) A obtiene 1 punto si la diferencia es **1**.
El(la) jugador(a) B obtiene 1 punto si la diferencia es **5 o 7**.
El(la) jugador(a) C obtiene 1 punto si la diferencia es **3 o 9**.

El primer jugador que consiga 7 puntos, gana.

Consejo: devuelve las cartas a los montones y baraja después de cada turno.

Chance Encounters ©EDC, 1995

Reproducible 24d (Spanish)

Evaluación de Productos Perfectos

Reglas para el juego de los Productos Perfectos

Gira las dos ruedas giratorias y multiplica los números.

El(la) jugador(a) A obtiene 1 punto si el producto es 0, 10, 20 o 30.

El(la) jugador(a) B obtiene 1 punto si el producto es impar.

El(la) jugador(a) C obtiene 1 punto si el producto es 4, 6, 8, o 12.

El(la) jugador(a) D obtiene 1 punto si el producto es 16, 18, o 24.

1. **Haz una cuadrícula** del resultado del juego de los Productos Perfectos.
   Usa el espacio de abajo o una hoja de papel aparte.

2. **Colorea o aplica** un código a la cuadrícula para mostrar de qué manera puede
   conseguir puntos cada jugador.

3. **Describe** de dos maneras la probabilidad de ganar puntos de cada jugador:
   con fracciones, decimales, porcentajes o razones.

   Jugador A:_____   Jugador B:_____

   Jugador C:_____   Jugador D:_____

4. **Explica** por qué el juego es justo o injusto.

Evaluación de Sumas Ocultas

1. Completa la cuadrícula del resultado del juego de las Sumas Ocultas.

Reglas del juego de las Sumas Ocultas

Gira las dos ruedas giratorias y suma los números.

Rueda #1   Rueda #2

A consigue 1 pt. cuando la suma es 4, 5, 6 o 7.

B consigue 1 pt. cuando la suma es 8, 9 o 10.

C consigue 1 pt. cuando la suma es 11, 12 o 13.

Cuadrícula del resultado de las Sumas Ocultas

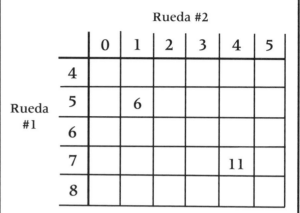

Rueda #1 \ Rueda #2	0	1	2	3	4	5
4						
5		6				
6						
7					11	
8						

2. Cambia las reglas para hacer el juego **justo**. Colorea o aplica un código a la cuadrícula para mostrar cómo puede conseguir puntos cada jugador.

Tus nuevas reglas:

Gira las ruedas giratorias y suma los números.

El(la) jugador(a) A consigue 1 punto cuando la suma es _____.

El(la) jugador(a) B consigue 1 punto cuando la suma es _____.

El(la) jugador(a) C consigue 1 punto cuando la suma es _____.

3. Describe de dos maneras la probabilidad de ganar puntos de cada jugador(a): con fracciones, decimales, porcentajes o razones.

A:_____   B:_____   C:_____

4. Describe cómo has cambiado las reglas para hacer el juego justo.

5. Extensión: Halla otra forma de hacer el juego justo.

De números a cuadrículas

Esta hoja enumera 6 probabilidades diferentes de ganar en los juegos.

1. Rellena las casillas de las cuadrículas para mostrar cada probabilidad.

A. $\dfrac{16}{36}$

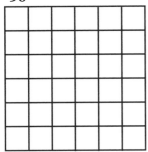

B. 25%

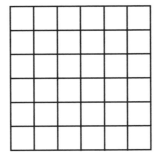

Ejemplo

$\dfrac{1}{6}$

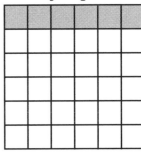

C. 3 de 4

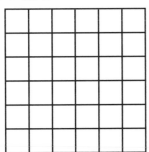

D. $\dfrac{1}{3}$

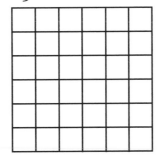

E. ,50

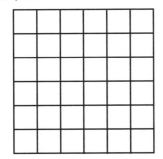

F. 6 de 18

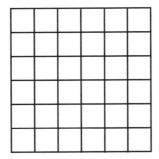

2. Clasifica las cuadrículas de la mayor probabilidad de ganar a la menor probabilidad de ganar. (Mayor = 1)

A_____   B_____   C_____   D_____   E_____   F_____

3. En cada una de las cuadrículas, ¿cuál es la probabilidad de *no* ganar?

A_____   B_____   C_____   D_____   E_____   F_____

Clasifica las cuadrículas

*Éstas son cuadrículas de probabilidad correspondientes a cuatro juegos desfavorables.
Si tú fueras Andrés, ¿a cuál de estos juegos te gustaría jugar?*

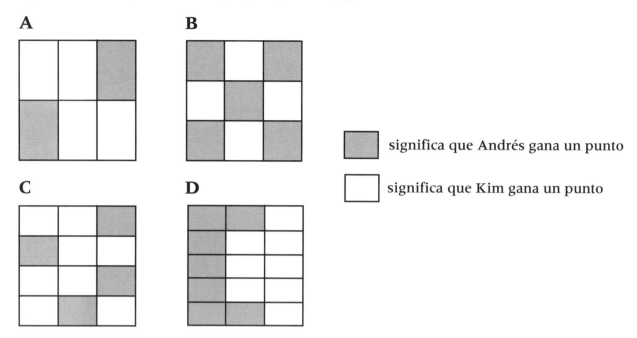

A   **B**

significa que Andrés gana un punto

significa que Kim gana un punto

C   **D**

1. Describe por lo menos de dos maneras diferentes la probabilidad de Andrés de conseguir un punto en cada juego. Usa fracciones, decimales, porcentajes o razones.

   A:_____   B:_____

   C:_____   D:_____

2. Clasifica las cuadrículas de "La mejor para Andrés" a "La peor para Andrés" (Mejor = 1).

   A_____   B_____   C_____   D_____

3. ¿Qué razonamiento has seguido para clasificar las cuadrículas?

4. En la otra cara de esta hoja, haz una cuadrícula que sea *mejor* para Andrés que el *segundo mejor* juego, pero *no tan bueno como* el *mejor* juego.

¿Es justo este juego de alta puntuación?

Reglas para el Juego de la Super Resta:

Tira dos dados. Resta el número menor al número mayor.

El jugador A obtiene 30 puntos si la diferencia es **0 or 5**.

El jugador B obtiene 10 puntos si la diferencia es **1, 2 or 3**.

El jugador C obtiene 45 puntos si la diferencia es **4**.

Juega 18 veces. Gana el jugador que consigue más puntos.

---

1. Haz una cuadrícula del resultado en una hoja de papel aparte para calcular la probabilidad que tiene cada jugador de conseguir puntos en el **Juego de la Super Resta**.

2. Completa la tabla de abajo.

Juga-dores(as)	Probabilidad de conseguir puntos en un turno	Número de veces que se espera que cada jugador(a) consiga puntos en 18 turnos	Número de puntos que puede obtener cada jugador(a) en un turno	Número total de puntos previstos en 18 turnos
A	$\frac{8}{36}$	4	30	120
B			10	
C			45	

3. ¿Es un juego justo o injusto? ¿Por qué? Si el juego es injusto, ¿cómo cambiarías el número de puntos que puede anotarse cada jugador(a) para hacerlo justo?

4. Si el(la) jugador(a) A consigue 6 puntos en un turno, ¿cuántos puntos les asignarías a cada uno de los otros jugadores para hacer el juego justo? ¿Por qué?

5. Piensa tu propio sistema de puntuación para convertir este juego en un juego justo.

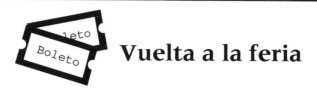

Vuelta a la feria

Usa lo que has aprendido en las Secciones 2 y 3 para analizar los Juegos de la feria de la Lección 1.

1. ¿Cuál es la probabilidad de ganar en la caseta de La Moneda y el Dado y en la caseta Sólo Jóvenes? Describe la probabilidad de ganar usando fracciones, decimales, porcentajes o razones.

2. Muestra tu probabilidad de ganar en cada una de las 6 casetas (A-F) en la línea de probabilidad de abajo.

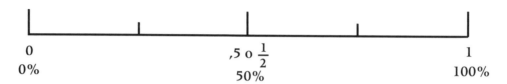

```
0            ,5 o ½           1
0%            50%           100%
```

3. Algunos de los propietarios de las casetas quieren aumentar el número de boletos que pueden ganar los jugadores en un turno. Quieren que los los jugadores ganen aproximadamente 24 boletos en 12 turnos. ¿Cuántos boletos debe dar cada caseta cuando un jugador gana un turno?

   Completa la tabla de abajo.

Caseta	Probabilidad teórica de ganar en 1 turno	Número de veces que esperasganar en 12 turnos	Número de boletos que puedes ganar en 1 turno	Número de boletos que esperas conseguir en 12 turnos
A. Pase Adelante	$\frac{1}{2}$ o ,5	6	4	24
B. 3 de la Suerte				
C. Pares o Impares				
D. Elige un Número				
E. Moneda y Dado				
F. Sólo Jóvenes				

4. Extensión: halla otra manera de hacer las casetas igualmente justas.

Simulación de golf en miniatura ✸

Rojo / Amarillo	1	2	3	4	5	6
1	¡Hoyo en Uno! (1)	Fallas por una Milla (5)	Putt, Putt Putt (3)	Al Agua (4)	Fuera de Control (5)	Has Perdido el Toque (4)
2	Golpe Flojo (3)	¡Hoyo en Uno! (1)	Golpe Flojo (3)	Buen Golpe (2)	Golpe Perfecto (2)	Putt, Putt Putt (3)
3	Has Perdido el Toque (4)	Atascado Bajo el Faro (4)	¡Hoyo en Uno! (1)	Atascado Bajo el Faro (4)	Fallas por una Milla (5)	Fuera de Control (5)
4	Fuera de Control (5)	Sol en los Ojos (3)	Fallas por una Milla (5)	¡Hoyo en Uno! (1)	Putt, Putt Putt (3)	Buen Golpe (2)
5	Fuera de Control (5)	Golpe Perfecto (2)	Golpe Flojo (3)	Buen Golpe (2)	¡Hoyo en Uno! (1)	Golpe Perfecto (2)
6	Al Agua (4)	Buen Golpe (2)	Putt, Putt Putt (3)	Sol en los Ojos (3)	Golpe Perfecto (2)	¡Hoyo en Uno! (1)

INSTRUCCIONES

En tu turno, tira dos dados de colores diferentes y lee los resultados en la cuadrícula. El número en la casilla muestra cuántos golpes fueron necesarios para meter la pelota en el hoyo. Apunta ese número en tu tarjeta de resultados.

Por ejemplo, si Sal saca un 4 en el dado rojo y un dos en el dado amarillo, obtiene un Buen Golpe(2). Eso quiere decir que fueron necesarios dos golpes para meter la pelota en el hoyo. Su puntuación es 2.

Hoyo	Resultado de Sal	Resultado de Ann
1	2	

Buen Golpe (2)

Juega **18** hoyos. ¡El jugador con la puntuación *menor* es el ganador!

Reproducible 31 (Spanish)

Hoja de resultados

¡Manía Mini Golf!

Jugadores(as)

Hoyo				
1				
2				
3				
4				
5				
6				
7				
8				
9				
10				
11				
12				
13				
14				
15				
16				
17				
18				
TOTAL				

comienzo

Hoyo en Uno: anota 1 pt.

comienzo

Cinco intentos de meter la pelota en el agujero: anota 5 pts.

En el golf en miniatura, las puntuaciones *bajas* son mejores que las puntuaciones altas. El jugador que *menos* puntos tenga después de 18 hoyos, gana.

Simulación de béisbol

Rojo Verde	1	2	3	4	5	6
1	¡Jonrón!	Strike FUERA	Fly FUERA	Sencillo	Sencillo	Ground FUERA
2	Ground FUERA	Triple	Sencillo	Doble	Strike FUERA	Fly FUERA
3	Fly FUERA	Strike FUERA	¡Jonrón!	Doble	Fly FUERA	Ground FUERA
4	Sencillo	Ground FUERA	Strike FUERA	Ground FUERA	Fly FUERA	¡Jonrón!
5	Ground FUERA	Sencillo	Triple	¡Jonrón!	Ground FUERA	Strike FUERA
6	Fly FUERA	Ground FUERA	Sencillo	Fly FUERA	Triple	Ground FUERA

Reglas: en una hoja de papel aparte, dibuja un campo de béisbol.

- Cada jugador(a) representa un equipo de béisbol. En tu turno, tira dos dados y mira en la cuadrícula si tu bateador(a) batea. (Usa fichas o pequeñas piezas de papel para marcar la situación de tus jugadores en el campo.)

Sencillo: todos los jugadores avanzan 1 base. **Doble:** todos los jugadores avanzan 2 bases.
Triple: todos los jugadores avanzan 3 bases. **Jonrón:** todos los jugadores van a la base meta.

- Sigue jugando hasta que tu equipo haga 3 fueras. Entonces, el otro equipo batea. Una entrada se acaba cuando los dos equipos han bateado.

- Conforme juegas, anota lo que obtienes en tu hoja de resultados. No te olvides de apuntar el número de entradas.

Turno	Equipo	Fueras	Sencillos	Dobles	Triples	Jonrones	Carreras	Total por equipo
1	A	|||	|||		||		||	2
	B	|||									

Hoja de resultados de béisbol

Turno	Equipo	Fueras	Sencillos	Dobles	Triples	Jonrones	Carreras	Carreras Total por equipo
1	A							
	B							
2	A							
	B							
3	A							
	B							
4	A							
	B							
5	A							
	B							
6	A							
	B							
7	A							
	B							
8	A							
	B							
9	A							
	B							

Chance Encounters ©EDC, 1995

Reproducible 34 (Spanish)

Datos reales de juegos de golf en miniatura

Fuente: tarjetas de resultados de un campo de golf en miniatura en Carolina del Sur.

Número total de partidas jugadas: 43

Número total de hoyos: 774

Resultado medio: 40,3

Tabla:

Evento	Número de veces que ha ocurrido cada evento en 43 partidas (18 hoyos en cada partida)	Promedio por partida
Hoyo en Uno	85	1,9
2 Golpes	477	?
3 Golpes	159	3,7
4 Golpes	49	?
5 Golpes	4	?

Gráfica de resultados en 43 juegos reales

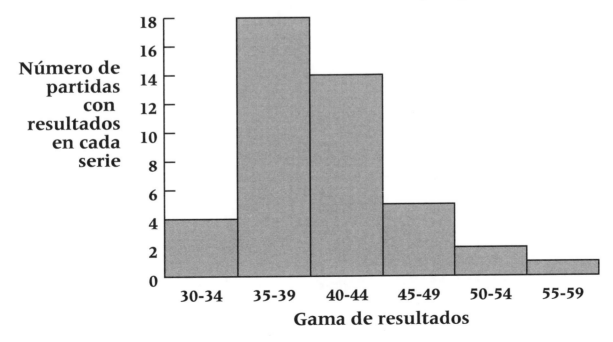

Número de partidas con resultados en cada serie

Gama de resultados

Datos reales de partidos de béisbol

Equipo: Toronto Blue Jays, temporada 1993
Número total de partidos jugados: 162
Número total bateos: 5.579
Promedio de carreras por partido: 5,23
Promedio de bateo del equipo : ,279

Tabla 1: Totales y promedios para cada evento

Evento	Número de veces que ocurrió cada evento en 162 partidos	Promedio de veces que ocurriócada evento por partido
Sencillo	1.038	6,41
Doble	317	?
Triple	42	?
Jonrón	159	?
Fuera (strike fuera, fly fuera & ground fuera)	4.023	24,83

Tabla 2: Probabilidad experimental de los eventos

Evento	Probabilidad experimental del evento como fracción de 5.579 bateos	Probabilidad experimental del evento como porcentaje de 5.579 bateos
Sencillo	$\frac{1038}{5579}$	19%
Doble	$\frac{317}{5579}$	6%
Triple	$\frac{42}{5579}$	?
Jonrón	$\frac{159}{5579}$	?
Fuera (strike fuera, fly fuera & ground fuera)	$\frac{4023}{5579}$	?

Formas para el juego de Lanzar

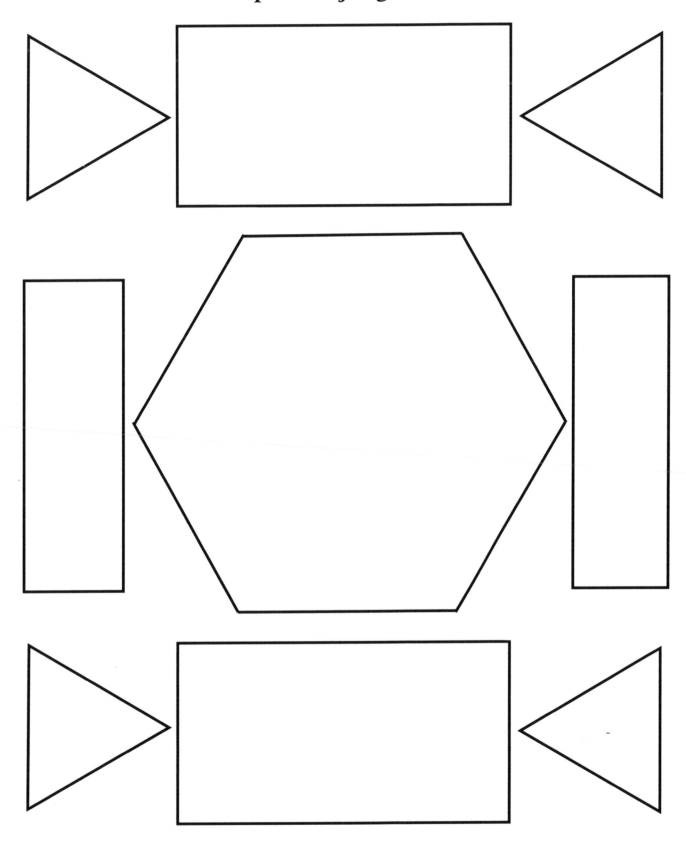

**Mapa tablero del
juego de Lanzar**

Sudamérica

©*EDC, 1995 Reproducible 38 (Spanish)*

Projecto final: Diseña una simulación

Qué necesitas hacer:	Fecha de vencimiento:
A. Planea tu simulación de juego. Elige una actividad real para la simulación. Describe tus ideas y cómo vas a recoger información en la *Hoja de Planificación del Proyecto*.	
B. Recoge información sobre la actividad real. Muest ra los datos que has recogido y explica cómo los recogiste. Escribe un sumario sobre lo que hallaste.	
C. Haz una línea de probabilidad. Usa tus datos para clasificar la probabilidad de los eventos de la vida real, de *poco probable* a *muy probable*.	
D. Diseña un tablero cuadriculado para la simulación de tu juego. Decide qué dos piezas del juego (dados, ruedas giratorias, etc.) vas a usar en la simulación y dibuja una cuadrí con el número apropiado de casillas. Por ejemplo, usa una cuadrícula con 36 casillas para dos dados. Rellena la casilla para hacer una simulación real. ¿Cuántas casillas vas a adjudicarle a cada evento? Colorea o codifica los eventos para que todas las casillas correspondientes a un evento tengan el mismo color o dibujo.	
E. Describe la probabilidad de los eventos en tu simulación. En tu simulación ¿qué probabilidad de ocurrencia tiene cada evento? Usa fracciones, porcentajes, decimales o razones para describir la probabilidad.	
F. Escribe las reglas. ¿Cuál es el objetivo? ¿Cómo consiguen puntos los jugadores? ¿Cuándo se acaba el juego? Puede que quieras diseñar una hoja de resultados.	
G. Prueba tu juego de simulación. Prueba jugando por lo menos dos veces y anota los resultados. Describe qué ocurrió cuando jugaste. Esta no es una prueba precisa de la simulación, pero te dará una idea sobre su funcionamiento.	
H. Junta las partes de tu informe y completa la Hoja informativa. Escribe una descripción de tu simulación y cómo la diseñaste.	

Chance Encounters ©EDC, 1995

Hoja de planificación del proyecto

☐ 1. **Describe el tema** *Consejo:* elige una actividad que conozcas bien.
   • ¿Qué actividad estás pensando simular?
   • ¿Qué experiencia tienes en la actividad que piensas simular?
   • ¿Por qué crees que el asunto va a interesarle a los demás estudiantes?

☐ 2. **Enumera un mínimo de 6 eventos diferentes que pueden ocurrir en la actividad real.**
   Trata de encontrar eventos que tengan diferente probabilidad de ocurrencia—eventos que sean muy probables, probables, poco probables y muy poco probables.

☐ 3. **Describe cómo vas a recoger información sobre tu tema.** Necesitas encontrar la probabilidad que existe en la actividad real de que ocurran diferentes eventos.
   Aquí hay algunas maneras de recoger información:
   • Entrevista a gente que sabe mucho de ese tema.
   • Busca libros que contengan estadísticas sobre tu tema, como las revistas de deportes.
   • Mantén un registro de tus propias experiencias y de las de tus amigos o familiares.
   • Observa la actividad personalmente o en televisión.
   • Busca en periódicos y revistas.

Hoja informativa del Proyecto final

1. ¿Sobre qué es tu juego de simulación?

2. ¿Cómo has recogido la información real? (Incluye los nombres de tus fuentes.)

3. ¿Cuál es la probabilidad de los eventos reales?
   Muestra la probabilidad de los eventos reales en la línea de probabilidad de abajo.

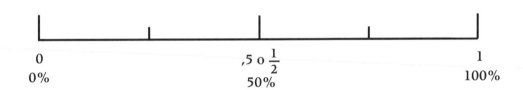

0	,5 o $\frac{1}{2}$	1
0%	50%	100%

4. ¿Cuál es la probabilidad de los eventos en tu juego de simulación?

Eventos	Número de casillas que asignaste al evento en tu cuadrícula de simulación	Probabilidad del evento en tu simulación (como porcentaje, razón, fracción o decimal)

Hoja de prueba de la simulación

Pon a prueba las simulaciones de tus compañeros/as de clase y diles qué te han parecido. Recuerda, tu trabajo es ayudar a tus compañeros/as de clase a mejorar sus juegos.

Nombre de la simulación:_____

1. ¿Qué te gusta de la simulación?

2. ¿Qué sugerencias te gustaría darle al diseñador?

3. ¿Es realista?

Algunas maneras de dar tu parecer:

> *Realmente me gustó cómo hiciste...*

> *Algunas de las cosas que podreias mejorar son...*

> *Tuve problemas en comprender lo que quieres decir al...*

> *La parte que a mí me pareció poco clara fue cuando dijiste...*
